OneNote 2016 and 2013

Studio Visual Steps

OneNote 2016 and 2013

www.visualsteps.com

This book has been written using the Visual Steps™ method.
Cover design by Studio Willemien Haagsma bNO

© 2016 Visual Steps
Author: Koen Timmers
Translated by Brigitte Sijm, *BRICKS Text & Translation* and Chris Hollingsworth, *1st Resources*.

First printing: December 2016
ISBN 978 90 5905 463 9

Resources used: A number of definitions and explanations of computer terminology are taken over from the *OneNote help function, Windows help function and Wikipedia.*

Do you have questions or suggestions?
E-mail: info@visualsteps.com

Would you like more information?
www.visualsteps.com

Website for this book:
www.visualsteps.com/onenote2016

Subscribe to the free Visual Steps Newsletter:
www.visualsteps.com/newsletter

Table of Contents

Foreword

As a web design teacher I am very committed to education in general and to e-learning in particular. Since I became a Microsoft Innovative Educator Expert in 2014 I have encountered hundreds of inspiring, international teachers. I have also come to realize how fantastic *OneNote* is. I now use the program to create the courses for all my classes.

OneNote is a very diverse program. It enables you to create a course as well as draw up a meeting report, a shopping list or book, and many other tasks.

I would like to thank a few people for making this book possible: my muses Rachel and Mauro; my sources of inspiration at Microsoft: Kirsten Panton, Mike Tholfsen and Nathalie Blondeel; Kurt Söser, Kyle Calderwood and Marjolein Hoekstra (*OneNote* MVP), always ready to lend a helping hand. Finally, I would like to thank Anthony Salcito (vice president of Worldwide Education Microsoft), Eve Psalti (Global Director, Audience Education Strategy, Microsoft) and Sonja Delafosse (Microsoft Audience Education Educator).

This book offers you a step-by-step method to work with *OneNote 2016* or *2013*.

Koen Timmers
www.timmers.me

The publisher welcomes all comments and suggestions about this book at the following email address: mail@visualsteps.com

Introduction to Visual Steps™

The Visual Steps handbooks and manuals are the best instructional materials available for learning how to work with mobile devices, computers and software applications. Nowhere else will you find better support to help you get started with *MacOS*, *Windows*, an iPad, iPhone, Samsung Galaxy Tab and various software applications.

Properties of the Visual Steps books:
- **Comprehensible contents**
  Addresses the needs of the beginner or intermediate user for a manual written in simple, straight-forward English.
- **Clear structure**
  Precise, easy to follow instructions. The material is broken down into small enough segments to allow for easy absorption.
- **Screen shots of every step**
  Quickly compare what you see on your screen with the screen shots in the book. Pointers and tips guide you when new windows, screens or alert boxes are opened so you always know what to do next.
- **Get started right away**
  All you have to do is have your computer and your book at hand. Sit some where's comfortable, begin reading and perform the operations as indicated on your own device.
- **Layout**
  The text is printed in a large size font and is clearly legible.

In short, I believe these manuals will be excellent guides for you.

Dr. H. van der Meij
Faculty of Applied Education, Department of Instructional Technology, University of Twente, the Netherlands

Visual Steps Newsletter

All Visual Steps books follow the same methodology: clear and concise step-by-step instructions with screen shots to demonstrate each task.
A complete list of all our books can be found on our website **www.visualsteps.com**
You can also sign up to receive our **free Visual Steps Newsletter**.
In this Newsletter you will receive periodic information by email regarding:
- the latest titles and previously released books;
- special offers, supplemental chapters, tips and free informative booklets.
Also, our Newsletter subscribers may download any of the documents listed on the web page **www.visualsteps.com/info_downloads**

When you subscribe to our Newsletter you can be assured that we will never use your email address for any purpose other than sending you the information as previously described. We will not share this address with any third-party. Each Newsletter also contains a one-click link to unsubscribe.

What You Will Need

In order to work through this book, you will need to have a number of things:

 Most importantly you need the English version of *Microsoft OneNote 2016* or *Microsoft OneNote 2013* on your computer.
It does not matter whether this program comes from the *Office* program package or the *Office 365* package.

Note: *OneNote* is installed by default on *Windows 10* and can also be installed for free on *Windows 8.1* and *7*, but this version has fewer features than the program from the *Office* suite. The same applies to the freely available web app. There are also versions available for iPad, Android tablets, iPhones and Android smartphones, but this book is not based on these versions.

 Your computer needs to have *Windows 10, 8.1* or *7* installed. *OneNote 2016* and *2013* will only work on computers with the *Windows 10, 8.1* or *7* operating system.

 A functioning Internet connection.

How to Use This Book

This book has been written using the Visual Steps™ method. The method is simple: just place the book next to your computer or laptop and execute all the tasks step by step, directly on your own device. With the clear instructions and the multitude of screen shots, you will always know exactly what to do. This is the quickest way to become familiar with *OneNote 2016* or *2013* and use the various programs and services it offers.

In this Visual Steps™ book, you will see various icons. This is what they mean:

Techniques
These icons indicate an action to be carried out:

 The mouse icon means you should do something on your computer by using the mouse. Also, the mouse will regularly be used for operations where you can use a trackpad, as well as a mouse. In the first chapter you can read more about using the mouse.

 The keyboard icon means you should type something on your keyboard.

 The hand icon means you should do something else, for example insert a USB stick into the computer. It is also used to remind you of something you have learned before.

In some areas of this book additional icons indicate warnings or helpful hints. These will help you avoid mistakes and alert you when you need to make a decision about something.

Help
These icons indicate that extra help is available:

 The arrow icon warns you about something.

 The bandage icon will help you if something has gone wrong.

 Have you forgotten how to do something? The number next to the footsteps tells you where to look it up at the end of the book in the appendix *How Do I Do That Again?*

The following icons indicate general information or tips concerning *OneNote*.

Extra information
Information boxes are denoted by these icons:

 The book icon gives you extra background information that you can read at your convenience. This extra information is not necessary for working through the book.

 The light bulb icon indicates an extra tip for using a program or service.

Website

This book is accompanied by the website: **www.visualsteps.com/onenote2016**
Check this website regularly to see if we have added any additional information, supplemental chapters or errata for this book.

For Teachers

This book is designed as a self-study guide. It is also well suited for use in a group or a classroom setting. For this purpose, we offer a free teacher's manual containing information about how to prepare for the course (including didactic teaching methods) and testing materials. You can download the teacher's manual (PDF file) from the website which accompanies this book: **www.visualsteps.com/onenote2016**

Prior Computer Experience

For working with this book, you should have some experience with *Windows* and simple word processing. Prior knowledge of *OneNote* is not necessary.

Other Office programs

More basic books are available on other programs in the *Microsoft Office* suite such as *Word* and *Excel*. For a complete list of all *Office* books, see the web page **www.visualsteps.com**

The Screen Shots

The screen shots used in this book indicate which button, folder, file or hyperlink you need to click on your computer screen. In the instruction text (in **bold** letters) you will see a small image of the item you need to click. The line will point you to the right place on your screen.

The small screen shots that are printed in this book are not meant to be completely legible all the time. This is not necessary, as you will see these images on your own computer screen in real size and fully legible.

Here you see an example of an instruction text and a screen shot. The line indicates where to find this item on your own computer screen:

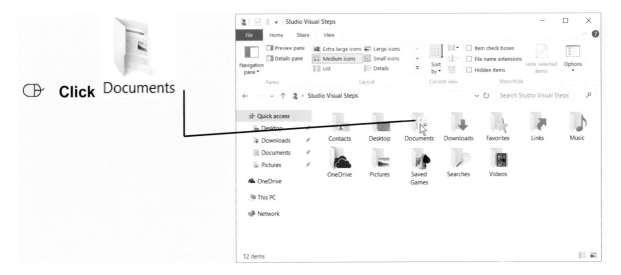

Sometimes the screen shot shows only a portion of a window. Here is an example:

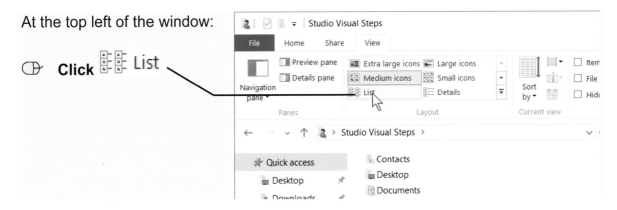

It really will **not be necessary** for you to read all the information in the screen shots in this book. Always use the screen shots in combination with the image you see on your own computer screen.

1. Starting a New Notebook

OneNote is more than a simple note-taking app. It is a comprehensive program that allows you to process texts, make drawings, share documents and a whole lot more.

If you are viewing the home screen of *OneNote* for the first time, it may seem a little daunting. *OneNote* contains some elements you may not be familiar with from other word processing programs such as *Word* or *WordPad*. *OneNote* provides more structure by dividing the notebooks, or documents in *OneNote*, into sections and pages. This helps you to organize and compile many different kinds of notes, such as to do lists, recipes, audio and video snippets and even books.

After this introduction chapter, the next chapter will explain how to make links between the different pages. In a recipe notebook for example, you could divide the starters, main courses and desserts into sections, and each individual dish could be placed on a different page. This will help you find a recipe much faster later on.

In this chapter you will create a new notebook and take a look at the structure of notebooks in general. In addition, you will learn various ways of saving data in *OneNote*.

In this chapter you will learn how to:

- start and set up *OneNote* for the first time;
- show and hide the ribbon;
- customize the *Quick Access* toolbar;
- create a new notebook;
- save and open a notebook;
- make, rename and delete a section;
- create, rename and delete pages;
- insert and delete text.

1.1 Start and Set up OneNote for the first time

You start and set up *Microsoft OneNote 2016* or *2013* in *Windows 10* as follows:

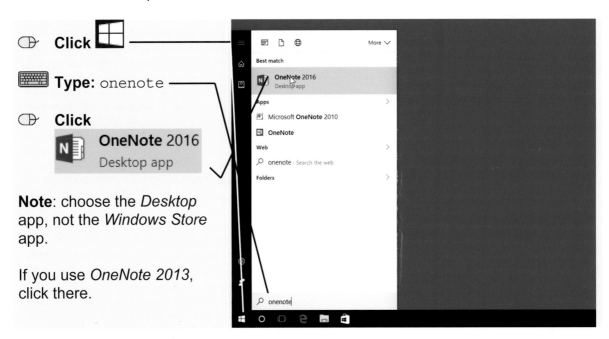

⊕ **Click** 🪟

⌨ **Type:** onenote

⊕ **Click**

    OneNote 2016
    Desktop app

Note: choose the *Desktop* app, not the *Windows Store* app.

If you use *OneNote 2013*, click there.

In *Windows 8.1* you open *OneNote* as follows:

⊕ **Click** 🪟

⊕ **Type:** onenote

⊕ **Click** [N OneNote]

In *Windows 7*:

⊕ **Click** 🪟, ▶ All programs, Microsoft Office, N Microsoft OneNote

OneNote is primarily focused on storing files online, so when you start the program for the first time it will ask for connection to the cloud. This enables collaborating with others on the same notebook.

A *Microsoft* account is required. This is an email address ending in outlook.com, hotmail.com or live.com combined with a password. It is also possible to connect a different email address to a *Microsoft* account. If you do not have a *Microsoft* account yet, you can create one on https://signup.live.com/signup

☞ **Click**

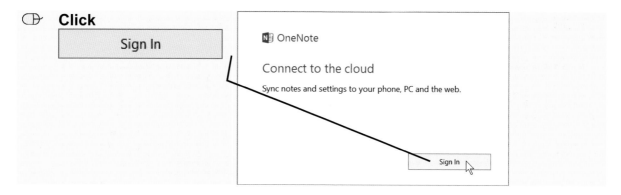

✖ HELP! I cannot see the windows.

You will only see the login screen the first time you start and set up *OneNote*. If you do not see this window, you can log in as follows:

☞ **Click** Sign in

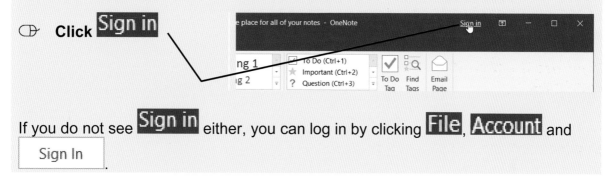

If you do not see Sign in either, you can log in by clicking File, Account and

Sign In .

✖ HELP! I do not want to log in.

It is also possible to work with *OneNote* without logging in. In that case, you can simply close the login window. Please keep in mind that you may not be able to perform some of the procedures described in this book.

Fill in your *Microsoft* account and password:

⌨ **Type your email address**

☞ **Click** Next

⌨ **Type your password**

🖱 **Click** Sign in

If you do not want to sign in with your *Microsoft* account, close this window. In *section 1.9 Saving a notebook to your computer* you can read how to create a notebook without storing it online.

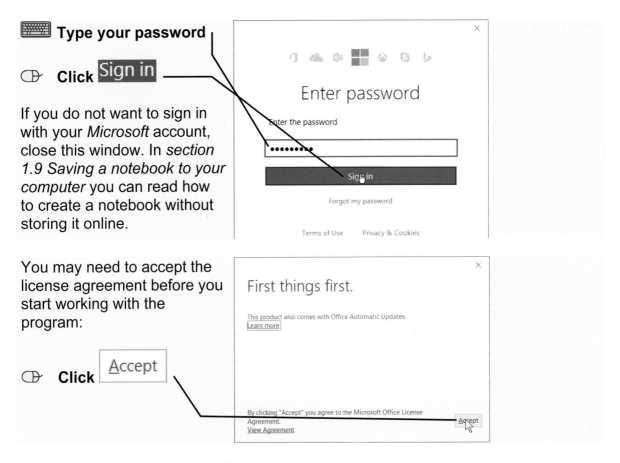

You may need to accept the license agreement before you start working with the program:

🖱 **Click** Accept

The *OneNote* window opens. The main elements of the program are:

The title bar shows the name of the program:

Quick Access toolbar:

Tabs:

The ribbon (not yet shown):

Notebooks:

Pages:

This worksheet shows a numbers of tips for using *OneNote*:

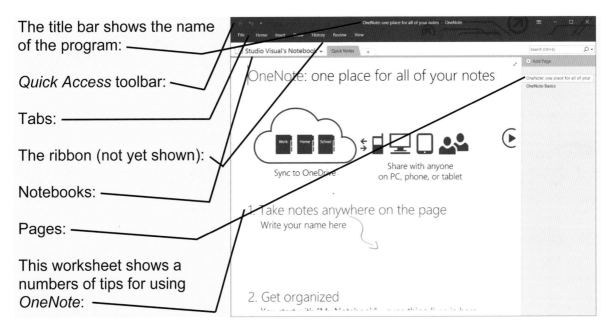

In the remainder of the book these elements will be used frequently.

1.2 The Ribbon

The ribbon is here to help you design and edit your notebooks. The various tabs contain an assortment of functions, divided by subject. When you open the program for the first time, the ribbon is hidden. You can show or hide the ribbon as follows:

 Click the tab

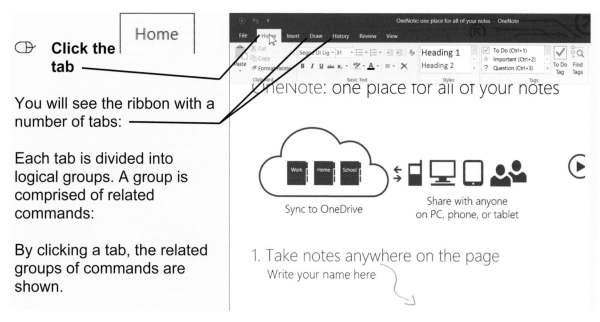

You will see the ribbon with a number of tabs:

Each tab is divided into logical groups. A group is comprised of related commands:

By clicking a tab, the related groups of commands are shown.

✂ HELP! My ribbon looks different.

Exactly which buttons you see on the tab will depend on the settings and size of your monitor. For example, on a high-resolution monitor:

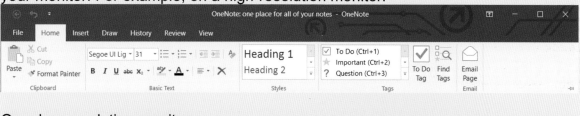

On a low-resolution monitor:

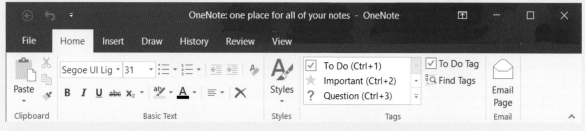

If you see a button that is only partially shown, just click it to see its icons and full text.

You will be using the ribbon quite often. It is therefore handy to pin the ribbon and keep it fully expanded:

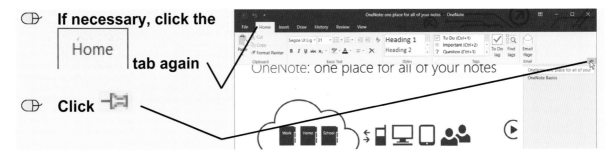

⊕   **If necessary, click the** | Home | **tab again**

⊕   **Click** 📌

The ribbon does takes up some space in the window. You can always minimize the ribbon when you temporarily need more workspace:

⊕   **Click** ⌃

The ribbon is now almost completely gone. You can expand (pin) the ribbon again:

⊕   **Click the** | Home | **tab**

⊕   **Click** 📌

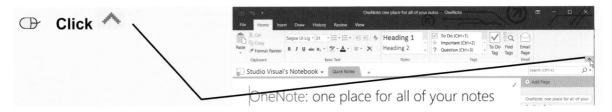

1.3 Adjusting the Quick Access Toolbar

If you want to use the ribbon for selecting a command, you usually have to click twice, both on the tab and then on the command. For frequently used commands, this can get a little tedious.

There is a special toolbar called *Quick Access* �icons. This toolbar lets you set buttons for frequently used commands that you can reach with just one click.

You see the *Quick Access* toolbar at the top of the *OneNote* window:

You can decide which commands will be included in the *Quick Access* toolbar. To add a command to the *Quick Access* toolbar:

☞ **Click** ≡

You see a menu with some frequently used commands:

☞ **Click**
Touch/Mouse Mode

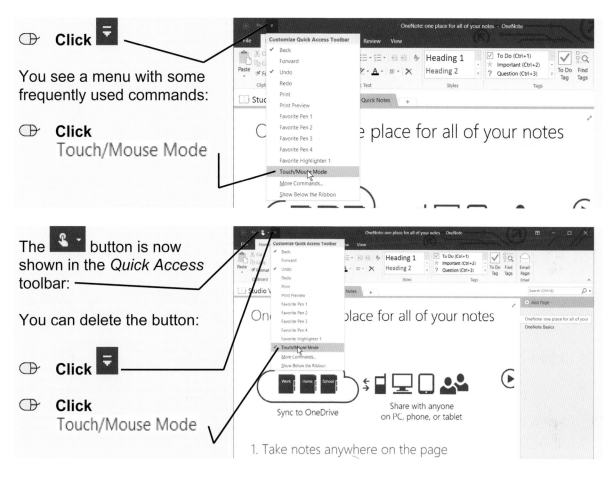

The ☝▾ button is now shown in the *Quick Access* toolbar:

You can delete the button:

☞ **Click** ≡

☞ **Click**
Touch/Mouse Mode

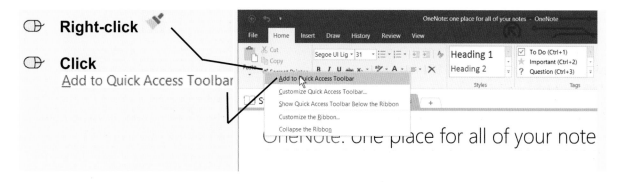

There is also another way for you to add buttons to the *Quick Access* toolbar. For example, the *Format Painter* button:

☞ **Right-click**

☞ **Click**
Add to Quick Access Toolbar

Now you see the 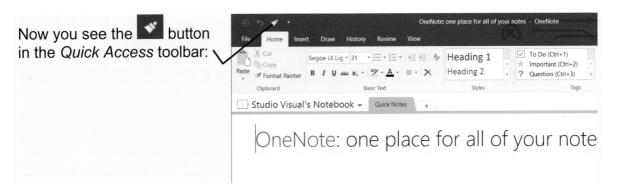 button in the *Quick Access* toolbar:

You can easily add more buttons later on in the same manner, for instance, whenever you notice you are using a particular option on the ribbon over and over again.

1.4 Creating a New Notebook

You now see the standard (default) notebook *OneNote* displayed the first time the program is opened. You can create your own notebook like this:

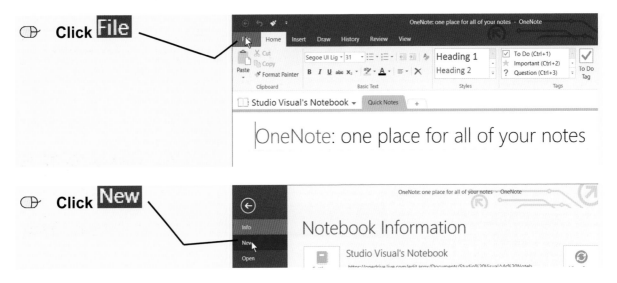

👉 **Click** File

👉 **Click** New

Now you have to make an important choice. Saving your document online or on your computer. When you save a document online, it is stored on *OneDrive*. This is also known as '*in the cloud*'. This makes it possible to share the notebook with others. Other people will be able to view and even edit this notebook.

Storing your document on your computer is more for personal use. In this book it is assumed that you will be storing your documents on *OneDrive*.

Here is how to do that:

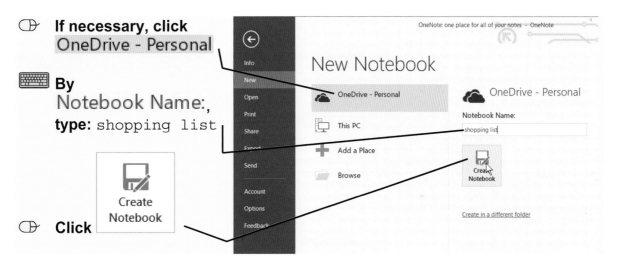

☞ **If necessary, click**
OneDrive - Personal

▦ **By**
Notebook Name:,
type: `shopping list`

☞ **Click**

Now that you have decided to store the notebook online, you will be asked if you want to share the notebook with others. You do not need to share the notebook for now. Sharing notebooks will be discussed in *Chapter 5 Sharing notebooks*.

☞ **Click** Not now

You see the new notebook:

The notebook is still empty:

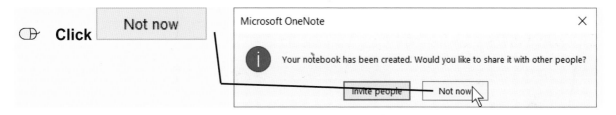

1.5 Sections

OneNote offers an interesting method for organizing and structuring your data. A *notebook* consists of sections which in turn consists of pages. Sections are accessed with the tabs above the notes. Pages are accessed by clicking the page title shown in the list on the right-hand side of the window.

A section can contain multiple pages and subpages. When you start a new notebook, you start with only one section containing a single page. The following examples show how sections and pages can be used to help you organize a notebook.

Sections:

Pages:

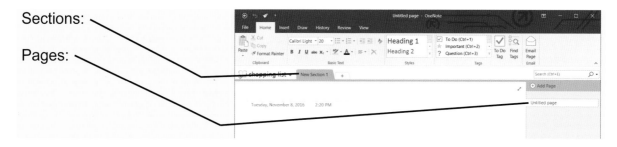

The section name can be changed:

👆 **Right-click the**

New Section 1

tab

👆 **Click** Rename

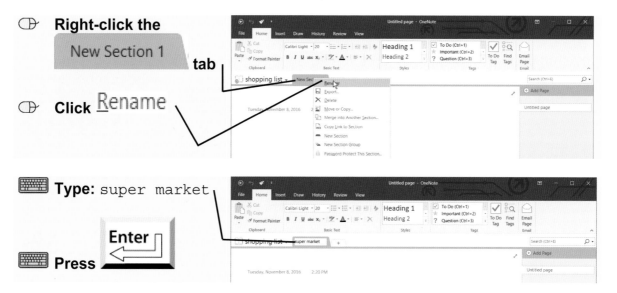

⌨ **Type:** super market

Enter

⌨ **Press**

💡 **Tip**

Changes with double-click
You can also rename a section by double-clicking it and typing another name.

Here you create a new section:

👆 **Click** +

⌨ **Type:** bakery

Enter

⌨ **Press**

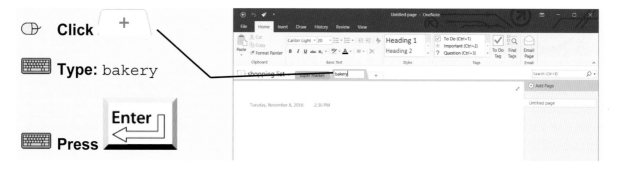

Each section is automatically assigned a different color. You can create as many sections as you like. In this example, you do not need the new section. You can delete a section like this:

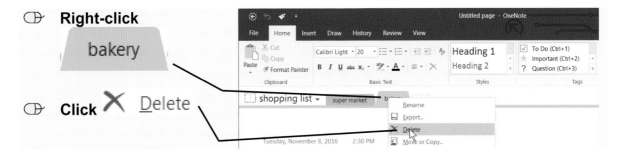

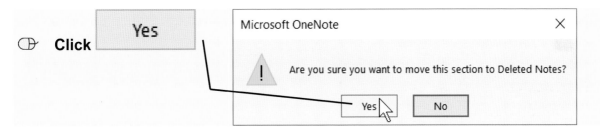

You will be asked whether you really want to delete the section:

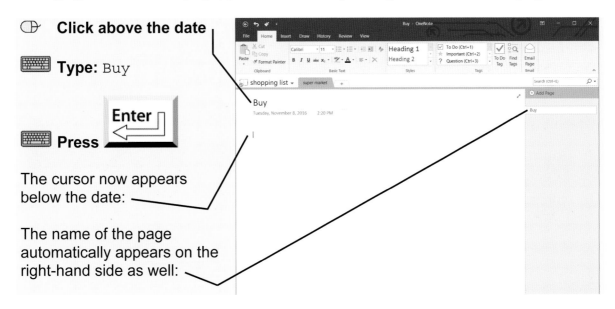

1.6 Pages

Within the sections, you can create pages. You give the first page a name or title. By changing the title of the page, you automatically change the name of the page:

☞ **Click above the date**

⌨ **Type:** Buy

⌨ **Press** Enter

The cursor now appears below the date:

The name of the page automatically appears on the right-hand side as well:

You can create another new page:

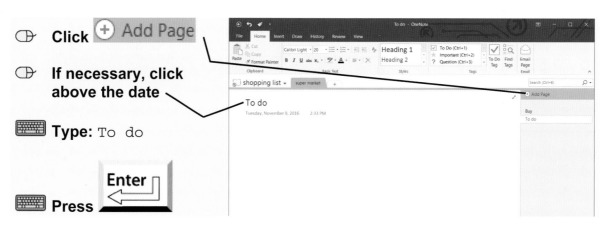

⊕ **Click** ⊕ Add Page

⊕ **If necessary, click above the date**

⌨ **Type:** To do

⌨ **Press** Enter

You can create as many pages as you like. The pages are listed on the right-hand side. You can change the order of the pages by dragging a page title up or down:

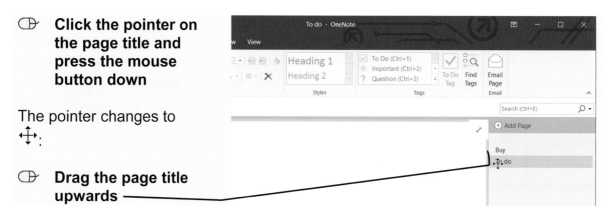

⊕ **Click the pointer on the page title and press the mouse button down**

The pointer changes to ↔:

⊕ **Drag the page title upwards** ——

💡 **Tip**

Changing the order of the sections
If you have created multiple sections, you can change the order of the sections in the same way.

You do not need this page anymore. You can delete the page:

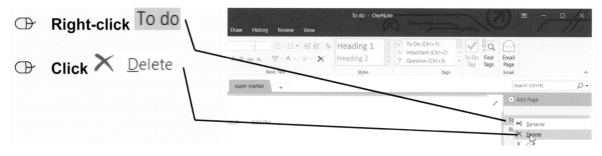

⊕ **Right-click** To do

⊕ **Click** ✕ Delete

The following section explains how to add text to the notebook.

1.7 Adding Text

It takes a moment to get used to entering text in *OneNote*. It is a bit different from what you are used to in other word processing programs such as *Word*. You can start anywhere in the window by clicking and typing immediately. As soon as you begin to type, a text box will appear around your text. You will find that after a short while this option not only has several advantages, it gives you a lot of freedom. Take a look:

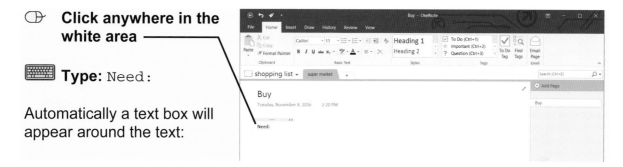

☞ **Click anywhere in the white area**

⌨ **Type:** Need:

Automatically a text box will appear around the text:

You can drag this box across the screen and place it somewhere else:

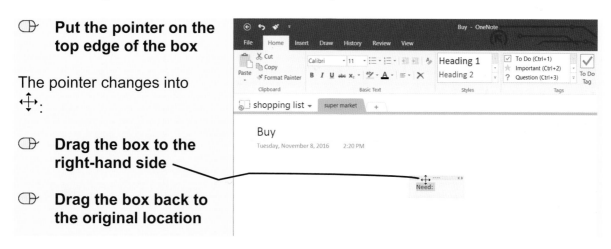

☞ **Put the pointer on the top edge of the box**

The pointer changes into ⬌ :

☞ **Drag the box to the right-hand side**

☞ **Drag the box back to the original location**

💡 **Tip**

Text against the left margin
It may feel uncomfortable to type just anywhere. After you have typed the page title

you can also click . Then when you start a new text, the text box will be pasted neatly against the left margin.

Now you can add some more text to the existing text box:

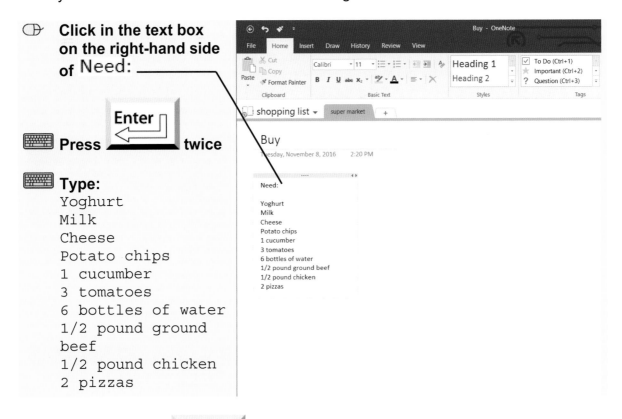

☞ **Click in the text box on the right-hand side of** Need: ——

⌨ **Press** Enter **twice**

⌨ **Type:**
Yoghurt
Milk
Cheese
Potato chips
1 cucumber
3 tomatoes
6 bottles of water
1/2 pound ground beef
1/2 pound chicken
2 pizzas

Every time you press Enter, a new line appears. The text box adjusts automatically to the length and width of the text.

You can create as many text boxes on a page as you like. As long as it is done next to the existing text boxes.

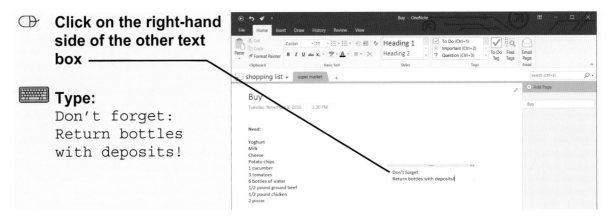

☞ **Click on the right-hand side of the other text box** ——

⌨ **Type:**
Don't forget:
Return bottles
with deposits!

You can also delete text boxes. As you move the pointer over the text, the box around the text appears.

Click on the top edge of the text box ——

Press **Delete**

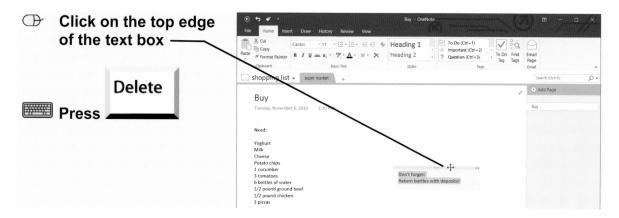

The frame and text are deleted.

1.8 Saving a Notebook

In *OneNote* you never have to save a notebook. There is no save button. That might feel a bit uncomfortable in comparison to most other programs. *OneNote* automatically saves your notebook while you work. When you close *OneNote* and open it again, it will automatically open the notebook that was open before you closed *OneNote*. This way you can immediately continue working on the notebook where you left off.

Take a look at how this works:

You can close the window:

Click ✖

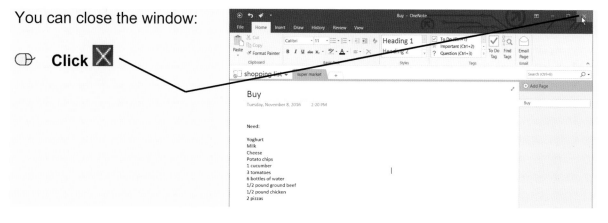

☞ **Open *OneNote*** 📶¹

Again you see the *Shopping list* notebook:

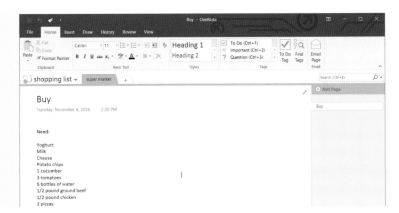

1.9 Saving a Notebook on Your Computer

This book primarily works with notebooks in *OneDrive*. However, if you want to store a notebook on your computer, you have to choose a few other options when you start a new notebook:

Click **File**

Click **New**

Click **This PC**

This button may be named 'Computer'.

By **Notebook Name:**, type: `Shopping list local`

Click **Create Notebook**

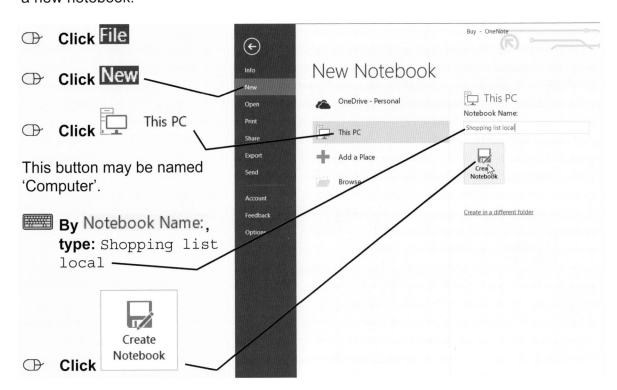

You may see a window with a message:

If necessary, click **Yes**

Please note:

Note that you have not chosen a specific folder on your computer. In this case, *OneNote* automatically saves the file in the *OneNote Notebooks* folder. This folder can be found in the *Documents* folder. From this location you can open your notebooks later on. More on this in the next section.

If you want to store a notebook in a different folder, click  Browse and open the desired folder.

The new notebook is now open:

In this example no further work is done on this notebook.

1.10 Opening Another Notebook

If you have already opened a notebook and want to open another, previously stored notebook, you do that in a slightly different way. Here is how to open the *Shopping list* notebook that is stored on *OneDrive*:

☞ **Click** File

☞ **Click** Open

You may see the notebooks from *OneDrive* already:

In this example, you open the notebook via the list of recent notebooks:

☞ **Click (if needed, the top one)**
  shopping list
  Studio Visual Steps's One...

In the above window, you see a number of options for opening notebooks:

 OneDrive - Personal   Click, and the notebooks stored on *OneDrive* will appear.

This PC   Click, and the notebooks appear which are stored on your computer in the *OneNote Notebooks* folder. This folder can be found in the *Documents* folder.

Browse   Click, and you can navigate via the window *Open* to a different folder where you previously saved a notebook on your computer.

Add a Place   Click and you can add a new location on *OneDrive* or *SharePoint*.

Now the *shopping list* notebook is opened again:

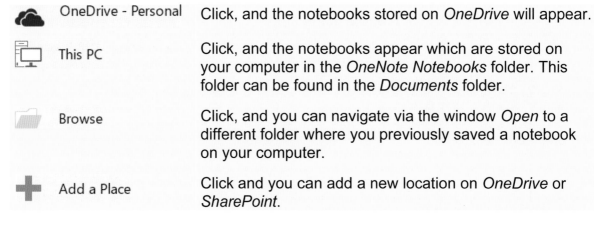

This chapter has shown you how to create and save a new notebook. Saving can be done both on *OneDrive* in the cloud, and on your computer. In the next chapter you can take a look at some of the formatting options available in *OneNote*.

☞ **Close *OneNote*** 🦶10

⬑ Please note:

If you are using *OneNote 2013*, then part of *OneNote* remains open. An additional toolbar button appears on the taskbar. Right-click on this toolbar button  and click Close to close this window as well.

1.11 Exercises

The following exercises will help you master what you have just learned. Have you forgotten how to do something? Use the number beside the footsteps to look it up in the appendix *How Do I Do That Again?* at the end of this book.

Exercise 1: Digital Cours

OneNote is an ideal application for collaboration purposes: digital courses, meeting reports, etcetera. In this exercise, you will create a new notebook for a digital course for which you can add other materials later on.

☞ Open *OneNote*. [1]

☞ Create a new notebook and save this to *OneDrive* with the name *Digital course*. Do not share this new notebook. [2]

☞ Change the name of the section and name it *Course*. [3]

☞ Create a new section and name it *Collaboration*. [4]

☞ Change the name of the page and name it *Chapter 1*. [5]

☞ Create three new pages and name these *Chapter 2, Chapter 4 and Chapter 3*. [6]

☞ Change the order of the pages in such a way that *Chapter 1, 2, 3* and *4* succeed one another. [7]

☞ Delete the page *Chapter 4*. [8]

☞ Add some text to the pages *Chapter 1* and *2*. (it can be anything) [9]

☞ Close *OneNote*. [10]

1.12 Background Information

Glossary

Microsoft account	An account can be created from *Microsoft* free of charge. This gives you access to various *Microsoft* services.
OneDrive	*Microsoft's* cloud service allows you to store files online.
OneNote	A *Microsoft* note-taking program that is part of *Office.* The program lets you gather information in a notebook and allows you to share it with others.
Page	A subdivision of a section in *OneNote.*
Quick Access toolbar	Special toolbar above or below the ribbon that is always visible. Here you can place frequently used commands.
Ribbon	The toolbar that contains commands in the top window of *OneNote.* The commands are divided into logical groups, sorted by tabs.
Section	A subdivision of a notebook in *OneNote.*
SharePoint	*SharePoint* is a *Microsoft* platform for exchanging information and collaborating online within a group or organization, as is often done on the Internet.

Source: OneNote help function, Wikipedia

What is OneDrive?

In this chapter the notebook was saved on *OneDrive*. But what is *OneDrive* anyway? *OneDrive* is a program to store files on the Internet. You can place documents on *OneNote*, open them from the Internet and share them with others. This is also known as 'the cloud'. The service offers 5GB free space to anyone with a *Microsoft* account. Additional storage space is available for a fee.

You can access files in *OneDrive* from the website http://onedrive.live.com. In *Windows 10,* the desktop version of *OneNote* also lets you use *OneDrive*, and *OneDrive* is included in *Explorer. Windows 8.1* also offers an app. For *Windows 7,* you can download a program from the http://onedrive.live.com website.

For access on mobile devices such as tablets or smartphones, you can download the *OneDrive* and *OneNote* app from the *App Store* or *Play Store*.

1.13 Tips

 Tip

Switching quickly between notebooks

You can easily switch between all opened notebooks using the selection list:

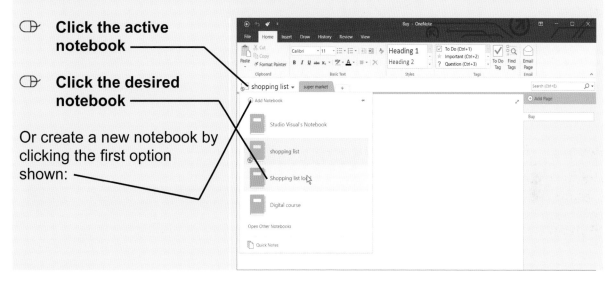

⬜▷ **Click the active notebook** ──

⬜▷ **Click the desired notebook** ──

Or create a new notebook by clicking the first option shown: ──

 Tip

Moving or copying pages and sections

Perhaps you want to use a section or page in another notebook as well. You can copy or move it. In this example, a section is copied. Moving a section or page and moving and copying a page are done in the same way:

⬜▷ **Right-click the section**

⬜▷ **Click**
    Move or Copy...

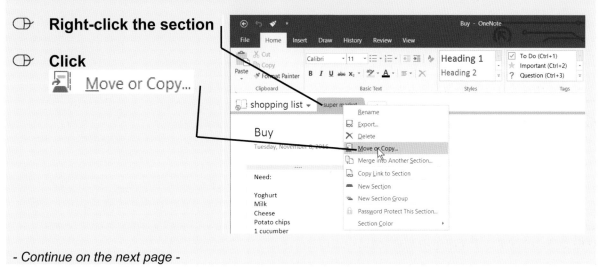

- Continue on the next page -

☞ **By** 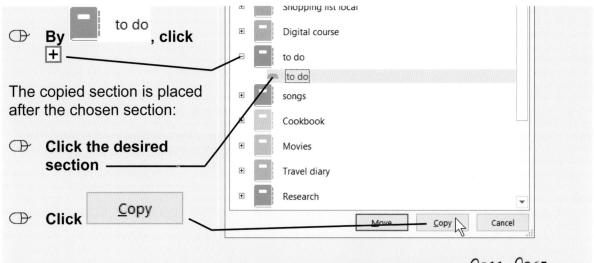 to do , **click** ⊞

The copied section is placed after the chosen section:

☞ **Click the desired section**

☞ **Click** Copy

☞ **Open the notebook to which you have copied the section** 👣**11**, 👣**65**

You can see that the section has been copied:

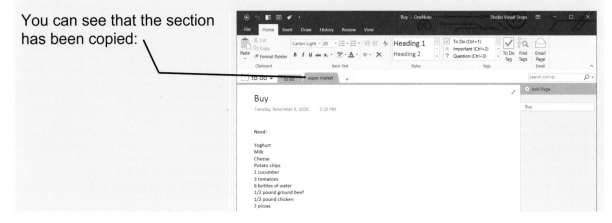

2. Page Layout and Text Formatting

Text formatting allow you to emphasize and clarify certain parts of a text. Adjustments to the page layout can also make things look better in a general sense. *OneNote* has to a large extent the same formatting options as *Word*, but some options have been specifically designed for *OneNote*.

You can also connect labels and tags to sections of text for search purposes. By using links, you can connect several pages together.

Page templates allow you to start a new page with pre-made layout and formatting included and sometimes even some skeleton content and structure.

In this chapter you will learn how to:

- apply and adjust text formatting;
- create links;
- use labels and tags;
- insert space;
- apply page layout;
- choose a different page display and zoom level;
- apply page templates.

 Please note:

In order to work through the exercises in this chapter, you will need to use the practice files made for this book. You can download these files from the website accompanying the book **www.visualsteps.com/onenote2016**. In *Appendix B Download the exercise files* you can read how to do this.

2.1 Text Formatting

Open *OneNote* on your computer:

 **Open** *OneNote*

You see the last notebook that was open when you closed *OneNote*. This is the standard setting in *OneNote* and allows you to start working right where you left off. During this chapter, however, you will be using a notebook from the practice files. This notebook contains a to do list with tasks and a few inspiring cases. You can use this practice file to become familiar with the layout options available in *OneNote* before you start creating your own notebooks:

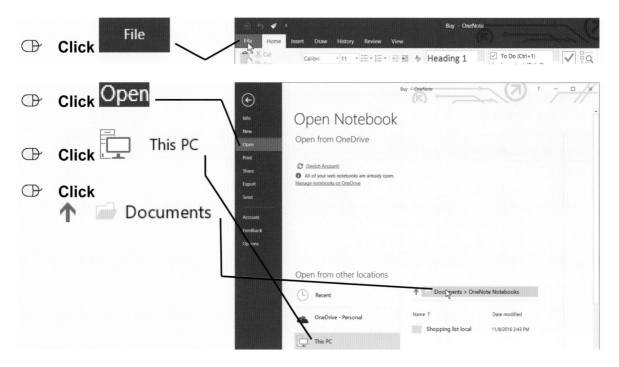

Now you see the *Open Notebook* window:

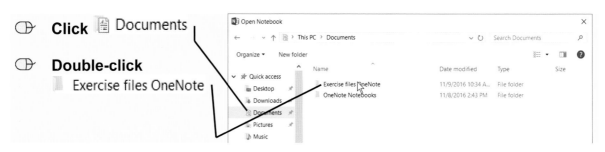

You can select the to do notebook:

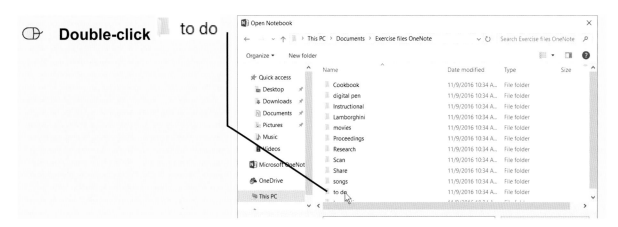

⊕ **Double-click** to do

Open the folder:

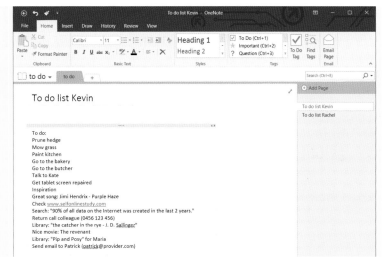

⊕ **Click** Open note

⊕ **Click** Open

Now you see the notebook:

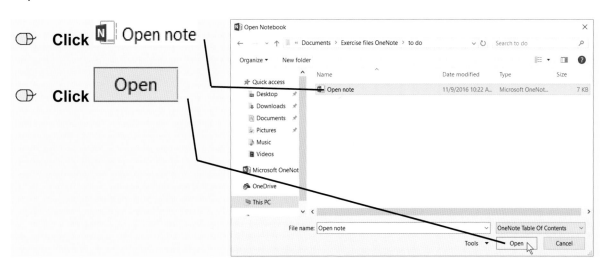

Below you see a brief description of the options available for text formatting. You probably already know these from other programs, such as *Microsoft* Word. To apply an option, first select the text you want to format by clicking it with or by dragging the pointer over it. Then click the option you want to use. The text is then formatted with the option you have chosen.

B   Make bold

I   Italicize

U   Underline

a̶b̶c̶   Cross out

A ˅   Change text color

ab ˅   Highlight

Calibri Light ˅   Change font

11 ˅   Text size

X₂   Subscript

X²   Superscript

≡ ˅   Aligning text (left, center, right)

≔ ˅   Bulleted list

≔ ˅   Numbered list

⇥≣   Increase indent

⇤≣   Decrease indent

A   Assign styles
Styles

🖌   Copy layout

You can practice with the familiar text formatting options and change a note's layout:

You can make the word
Paint bold:

☞ **Select the word** Paint
✂12

☞ **Click** **B**

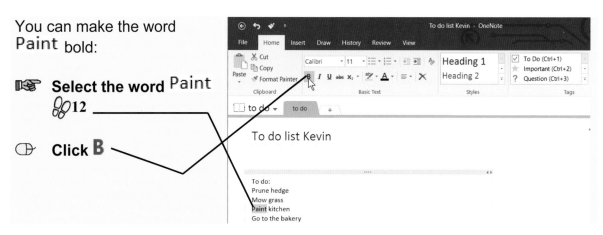

In the same way you can italicize, cross out, or give the text a color:

☞ **Apply the formatting as shown here**

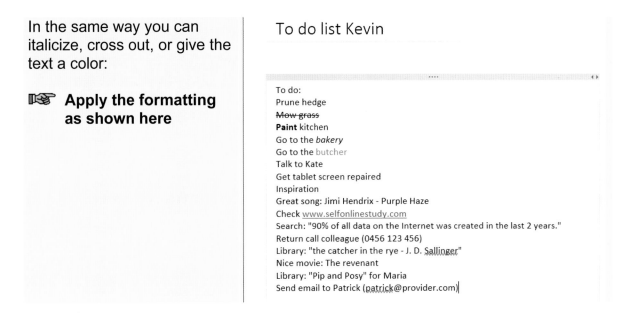

For lists it is useful to create a bulleted list and add a heading:

Start by making a heading:

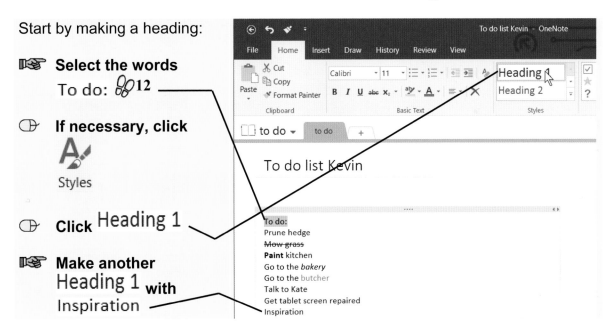

☞ **Select the words**
To do: 👣12

👆 **If necessary, click**

A̷
Styles

👆 **Click** Heading 1

☞ **Make another**
Heading 1 **with**
Inspiration

Make the bulleted list:

☞ **Select the text "Prune hedge … screen repaired"** 👣12

☞ **Click**

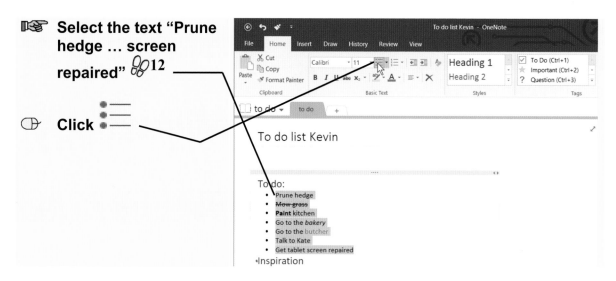

You can make a numbered list in the same way:

☞ **Select the text "Great song … (patrick @provider.com)"** 👣12

☞ **Click**

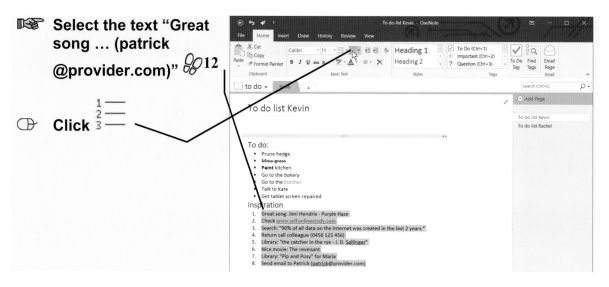

⮡ **Click outside the selection**

After adding the text, the note will look like this:

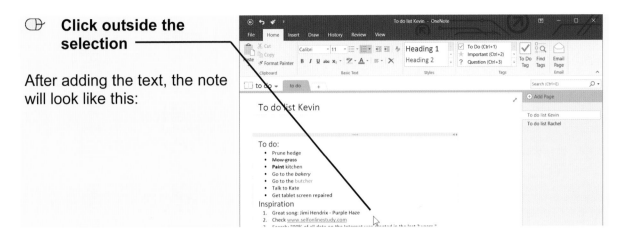

You have not made any changes yet to the page *To do list Rachel*. You will start doing this in the following section.

2.2 Creating Links

OneNote can also place links or hyperlinks between different pages and sections. This way with one click on a word or snippet of text you are immediately taken to the referred page. You can create a link from the page *To do list Kevin* to the page *To do list Rachel*. First add a sentence to the current note:

⮡ **Click the right-hand side of the last line**

⌨ **Press** [Enter] **three times**

⌨ **Type:** Check to do list Rachel

☞ **Select the text "Check to do list Rachel"** 👣 **12**

⮡ **Right-click selection**

⮡ **Click** Link... (Ctrl+K)

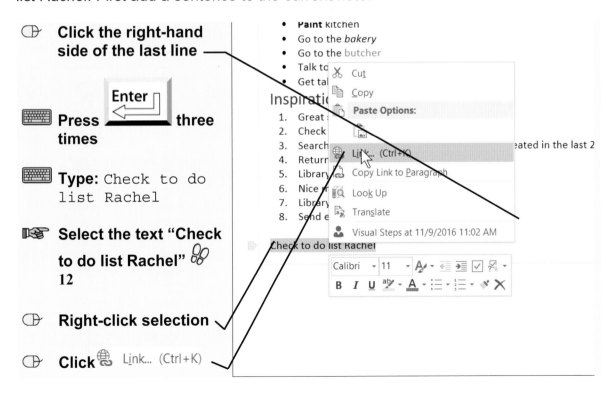

The window in which you create the link opens:

You can select the option for creating a link to another notebook:

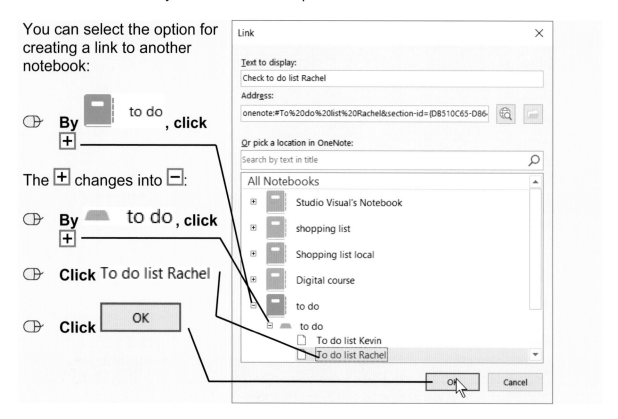

⊕ **By** [book icon] to do **, click** +

The + changes into −:

⊕ **By** [tab icon] to do **, click** +

⊕ **Click** To do list Rachel

⊕ **Click** OK

The link has now been made. The selected text turns blue. When you place the pointer on the link, a hand appears:

⊕ **Place the pointer on the link**

Now you see the hand:

⊕ **Click the link**

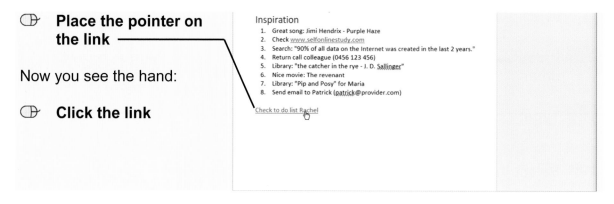

You are now on the page *To do list Rachel*:

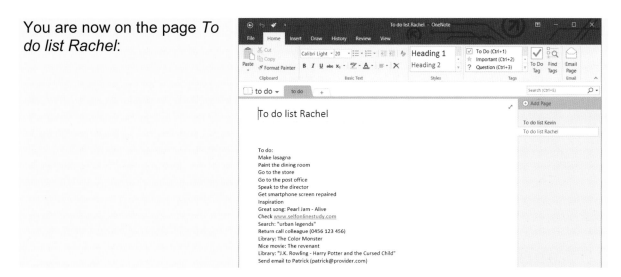

There is a second way of creating links that's even faster. By using the characters [[and]] a word is highlighted and the text is automatically converted to a link. The only condition is that the text is identical to the page you want to link to.

You can use this method to create a link from the page *To do list Rachel* to the page *To do list Kevin*:

Click the right-hand side of the last line

Press twice Enter

Type: Check [[To do list Kevin]]

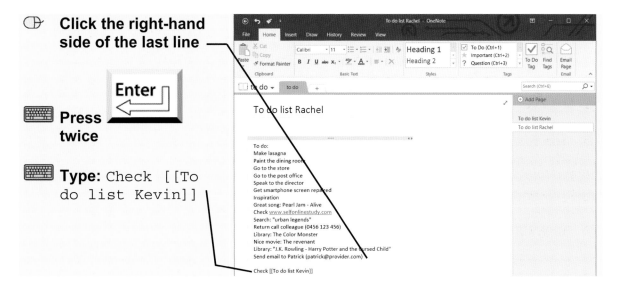

The moment you type the second] the link turns blue and becomes active. Take a look:

⊕ Click the link

Now you see the page
To do list Kevin.

2.3 Labels and Tags

OneNote allows you to attach labels and tags to words or sections of text. The labels form a sort of summing-up list or checklist. With tags, you can categorize text documents and attach priorities to the texts.
Learn how to add a task tag to the to do list:

☞ Select the text"Prune hedge ... screen repaired" 👣12

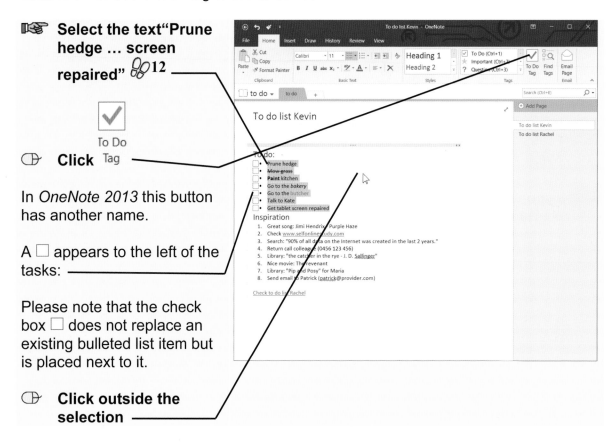

⊕ Click To Do Tag

In *OneNote 2013* this button has another name.

A ☐ appears to the left of the tasks: ———

Please note that the check box ☐ does not replace an existing bulleted list item but is placed next to it.

⊕ Click outside the selection ———

What makes task tags interesting is the ability to check off the finished tasks. This gives you a good overview.

☞ **Check the box ☐ by ~~Mow grass~~**

The check box changes into ☑:

☞ **Check the boxes ☐ by Go to the *bakery* and Go to the butcher**

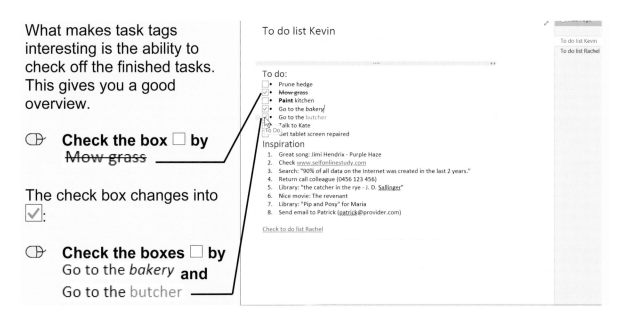

You can now add other labels, for instance the ♪ Music to listen to label:

☞ **Select the text "Great song ... Purple Haze" ✂12**

☞ **By Tags, click ▾**

If you see ?☑★, click.

You see all the different labels in the list:

☞ **Click ♪ Music to listen to**

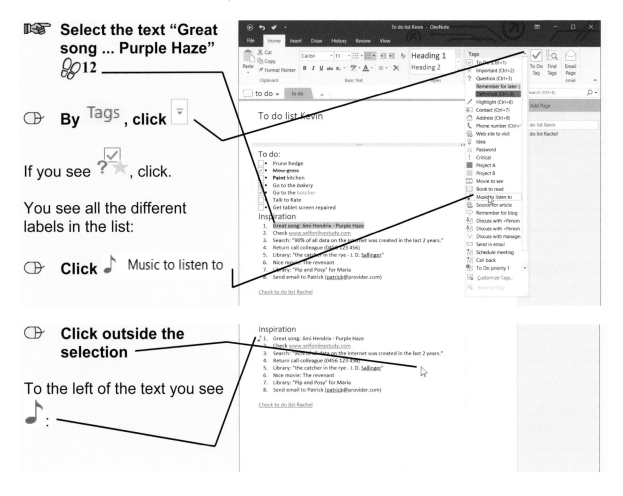

☞ **Click outside the selection**

To the left of the text you see ♪ :

As you have seen, the list includes various types of labels. Check these once again at your leisure. There are other labels you can add in the same manner. Try this out for the labels 🌐, 📞, 🎞 and 📖:

👉 **Add labels as shown here**

Inspiration
🎵 1.   Great song: Jimi Hendrix - Purple Haze
🌐 2.   Check www.selfonlinestudy.com
🌐 3.   Search: "90% of all data on the Internet was created in the last 2 years."
📞 4.   Return call colleague (0456 123 456)
📖 5.   Library: "the catcher in the rye - J. D. Sallinger"
🎞 6.   Nice movie: The revenant
📖 7.   Library: "Pip and Posy" for Maria
📧 8.   Send email to Patrick (patrick@provider.com)

You can delete labels like this:

👉 **Select the text "Great song ... Purple Haze"**

✂12

⊕ **By** Tags **, click** ▾

If you see ?⭐, click.

⊕ **Click**
   🎵 Music to listen to

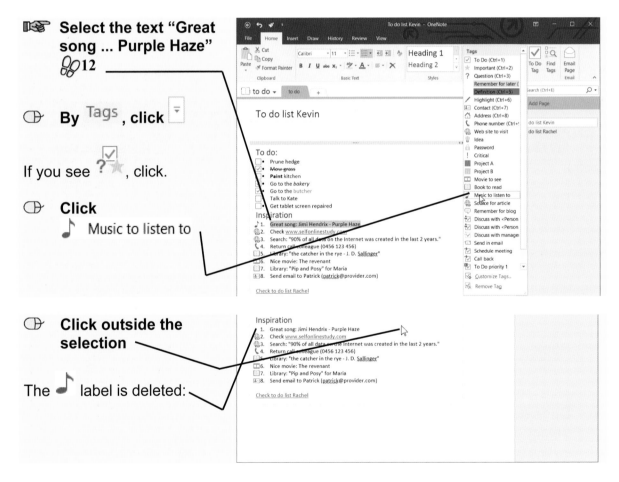

⊕ **Click outside the selection**

The 🎵 **label is deleted:**

It is also possible to search through the labels and tags. In this example all labels are put together on two pages, but you can also put tags in larger pieces of text, spread across multiple pages, sections, and even notebooks. In that case, a search function is useful for showing all to do's or other tasks.

First take a look at the *Tag Summary* pane:

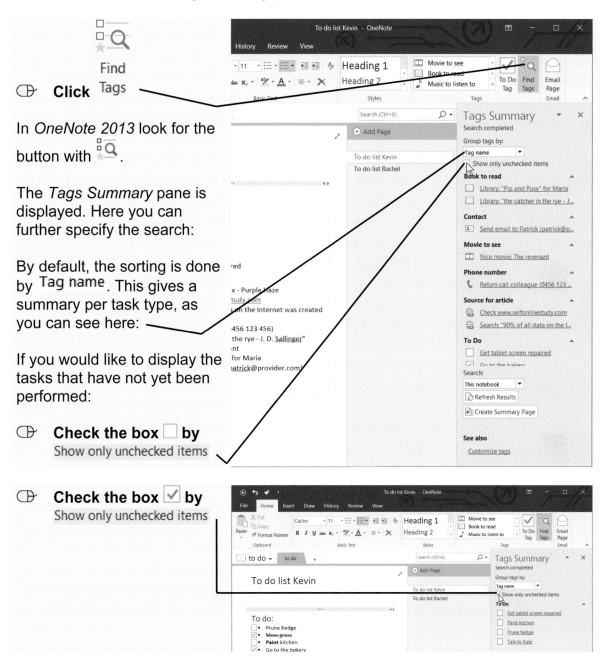

☞ **Click** Find Tags

In *OneNote 2013* look for the button with .

The *Tags Summary* pane is displayed. Here you can further specify the search:

By default, the sorting is done by Tag name. This gives a summary per task type, as you can see here:

If you would like to display the tasks that have not yet been performed:

☞ **Check the box ☐ by**
Show only unchecked items

☞ **Check the box ☑ by**
Show only unchecked items

Now all task tags are
displayed again:

You can also sort
alphabetically by task
heading or title:

👆 **By** Group tags by: **click**
   ▼

👆 **Click** Title

You can decide for yourself what the scope of the search needs to be, such as this
section, this notebook, all notebooks, and in addition, you can search the notes of
today, yesterday, this week and last week. By default, only this notebook is searched.
In this example, you choose to search last week's notebooks:

👆 **By** Search: **, click** ▼

👆 **Click**
   Last week's notes

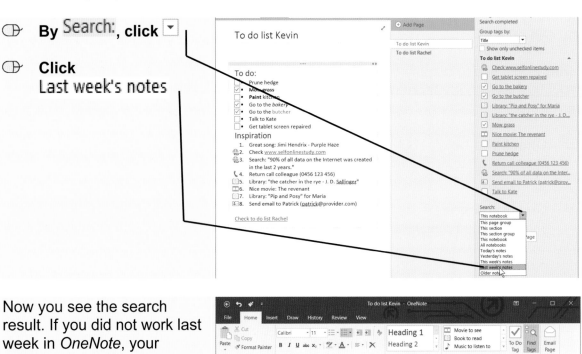

Now you see the search
result. If you did not work last
week in *OneNote*, your
search result will look
different:

Close the tag summary pane:

👆 **Click** ✕

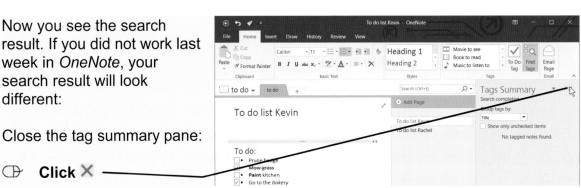

2.4 Inserting Space

OneNote contains an option for inserting space at any location you like. The difference with inserting enters in the text boxes is that space insertion works for multiple text boxes. It can also split a text into multiple text boxes. Later in this book you will learn how to add images and digital ink in *OneNote*. This feature will prove its value the more you use it. Inserting space only works horizontally. This option for inserting space also lets you do things in reverse, that is you can remove space when you do not need it.

☞ **Open the notebook *songs* from the *Exercise files OneNote* folder** 🐾[11]

You see the notebook and you can insert space:

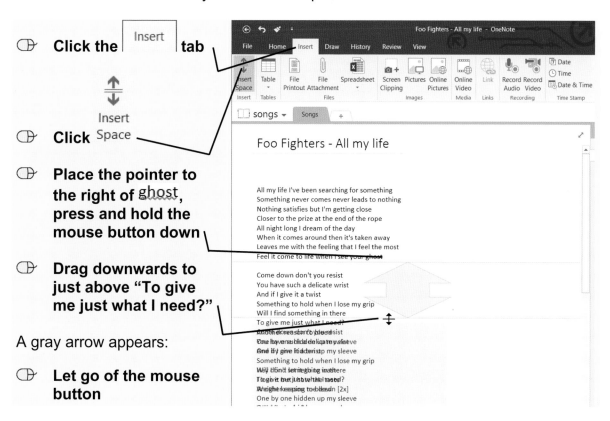

☞ **Click the** Insert **tab**

☞ **Click** Space

☞ **Place the pointer to the right of ghost, press and hold the mouse button down**

☞ **Drag downwards to just above "To give me just what I need?"**

A gray arrow appears:

☞ **Let go of the mouse button**

The text has moved down and the text box is divided into two text boxes:

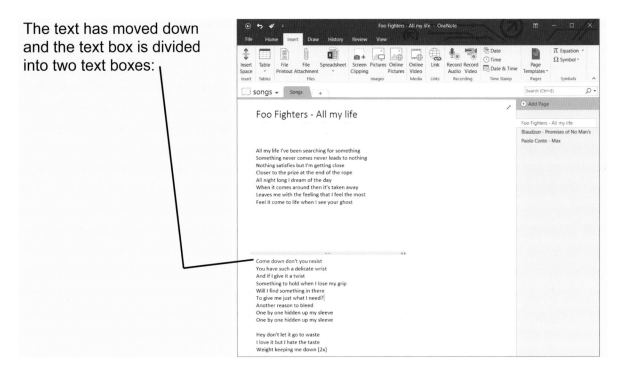

This space can also be removed again:

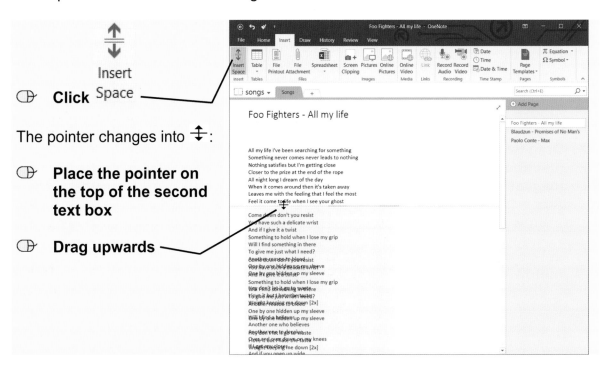

The space between the two text boxes is gone, but the text boxes will not be merged into one single text box:

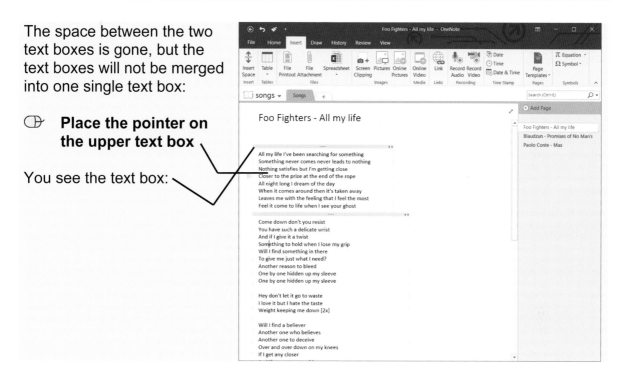

☞ **Place the pointer on the upper text box**

You see the text box:

Alas, it is not possible anymore to merge the two text boxes.

2.5 Page Layout

OneNote includes several options to adjust the page layout. Page layout, as the word already suggests, can only be applied to the active page. You can customize the page color, rule lines and page size. You start by changing the page color. You are now on the page *Foo Fighters - All my life*:

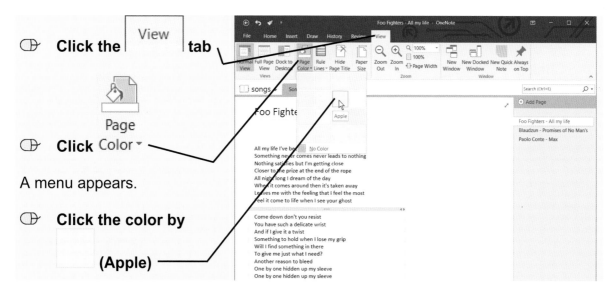

☞ **Click the** View **tab**

☞ **Click** Page Color ▾

A menu appears.

☞ **Click the color by**

(Apple)

💡 Tip

No color

Have you applied a color to the page, but now decide not to, just click No Color and you will return to the default white background color.

The page background now has a color: ⎯⎯⎯⎯⎯

Please note: the other pages will retain their white background color.

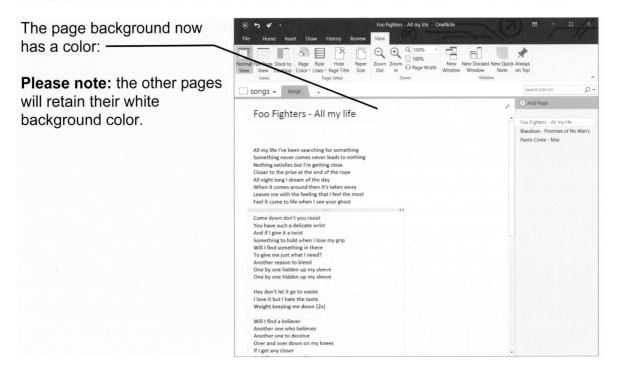

Rule lines mimic a classic note paper page and sometimes make a note easier to read. Apply rule lines to the page *Blaudzun - Promises of No Man's land*:

Click Blaudzun - Promises of No

Click [rule lines icon]

The rule lines appear directly:

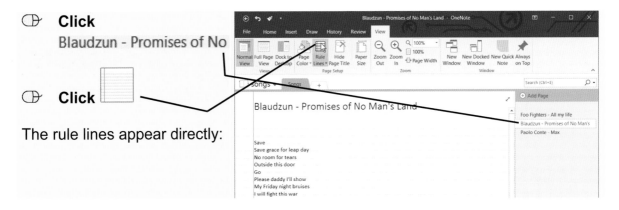

More types of rule lines are available:

Click Rule Lines ▾

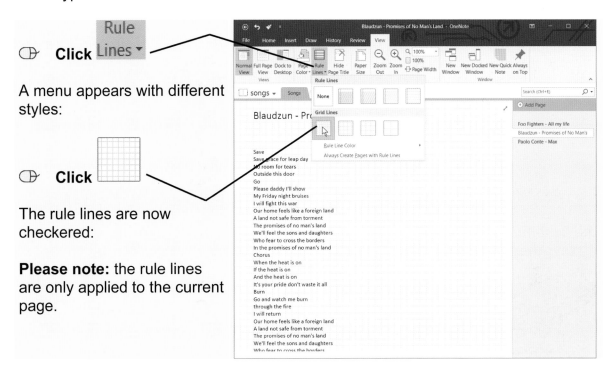

A menu appears with different styles:

Click

The rule lines are now checkered:

Please note: the rule lines are only applied to the current page.

OneNote automatically displays the page title above the note and in the right-hand column. You can hide this, if you want. Take a look at the page Paolo Conte - Max:

Click Paolo Conte - Max

Hide

Click Page Title

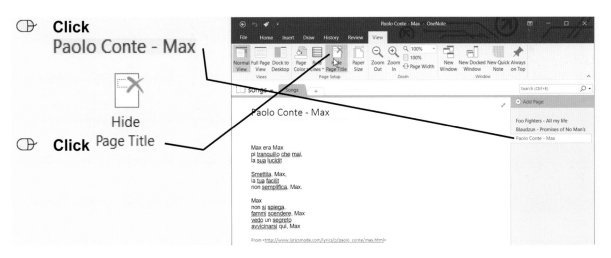

You will be asked for a confirmation:

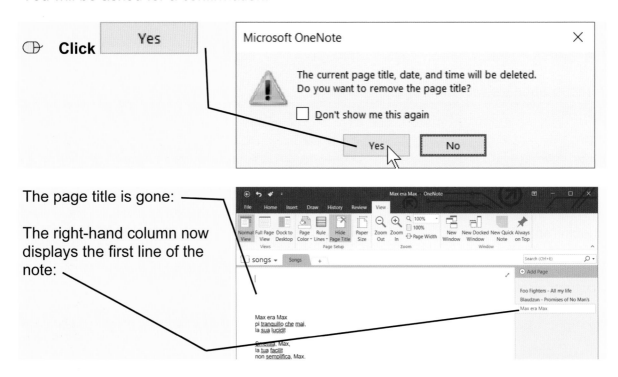

⊕ **Click** Yes

The page title is gone:

The right-hand column now displays the first line of the note:

The paper size can be adjusted in *OneNote* to various formats. Here is how to adjust the paper size of the current page:

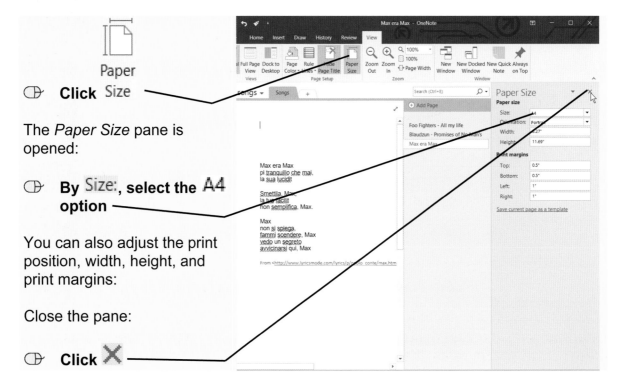

⊕ **Click** Paper Size

The *Paper Size* pane is opened:

⊕ **By** Size:, **select the** A4 **option**

You can also adjust the print position, width, height, and print margins:

Close the pane:

⊕ **Click** ✕

Please note:

If you adjust the paper size format, the text may move on the page.

2.6 Page Display

Since you often look at the notes on the screen itself, the current display of the page can be important. If things seem a bit too cluttered, you can easily switch to a larger page view in *OneNote*. This does not change anything in the layout, but just makes it easier to view your notebook. By default, the note is displayed in the Normal view. In this example, you will change that to the Full page view:

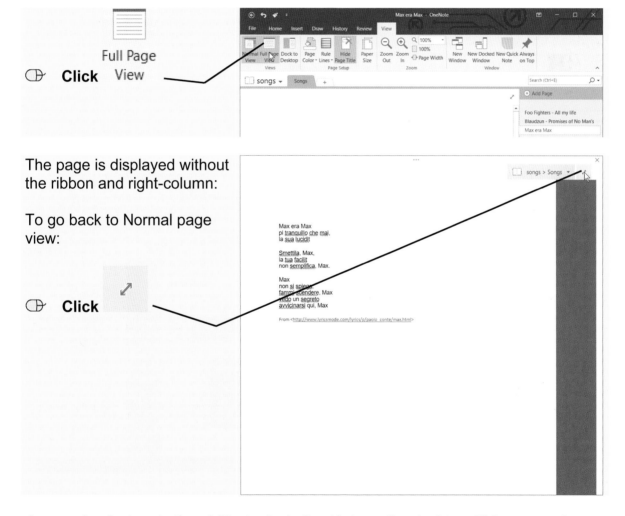

The page is displayed without the ribbon and right-column:

To go back to Normal page view:

A very nice feature is the ability to dock *OneNote* on the desktop. This means that *OneNote* is fixed on the right-hand side of the desktop. Even if you open and use other computer programs, they will not overlap the *OneNote* window.

You can practice docking *OneNote* on the desktop while a website is opened:

☞ **Open the website www.songlyrics.com in an Internet browser, such as Edge or Internet Explorer**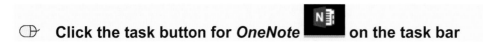

The *OneNote* window is now behind the browser window. You can let it come to the foreground again:

⬚ **Click the task button for *OneNote***  **on the task bar**

Now dock the window:

Dock to
⬚ **Click** Desktop

The *OneNote* window is now next to the Internet browser. When you open another program, such as *Word*, *OneNote* will not overlap that program.

Now turn off docking again and go back to normal view:

⬚ **Click** ↗

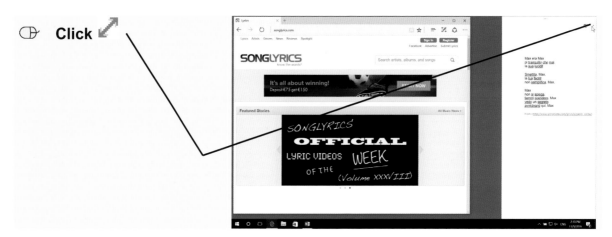

Now you see the normal view again:

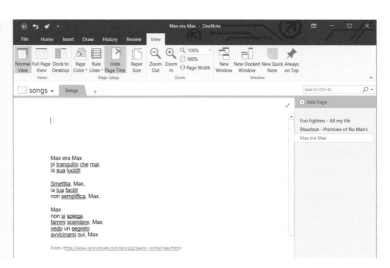

☞ **Close the window of your Internet browser** ✎[10]

2.7 Setting Zoom level

Finally, you can take a look at the zoom options in *OneNote*. Zooming allows you to enlarge or reduce a page or a part of it. First you zoom in on the page:

⊕ **If necessary, click the** | View | **tab**

⊕ **Click** 🔍 **Zoom In three times**

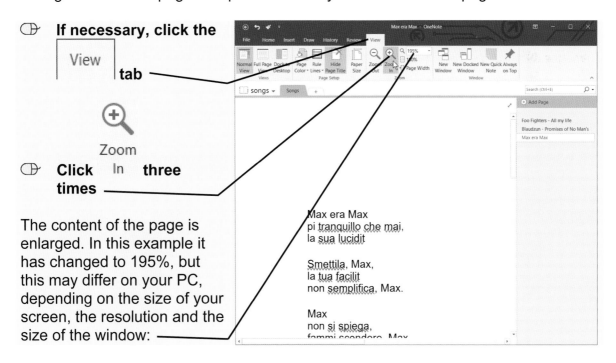

The content of the page is enlarged. In this example it has changed to 195%, but this may differ on your PC, depending on the size of your screen, the resolution and the size of the window:

In the same way you can

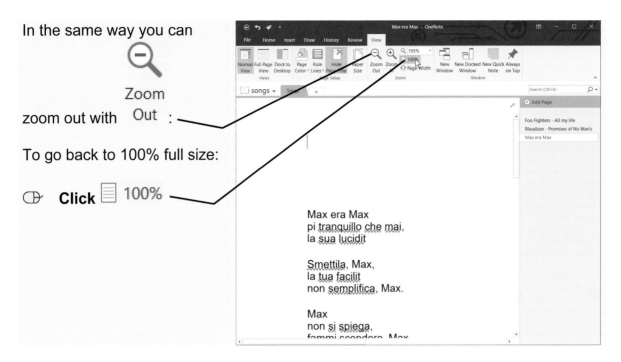

zoom out with Zoom Out :

To go back to 100% full size:

⊕ **Click** 📄 100%

You can also set the zoom percentage manually:

⊕ **By** 🔍 **, click** ▼

⊕ **Click** 75%

You see the page at 75%:

On the right-hand side of the page you now see a gray area. This indicates that the page width is not fully used.

You can also zoom out to the page width. The page then takes the full available page width and eliminates the gray area again. The page width is often 100%, but not always. This depends on the width of the sidebar.

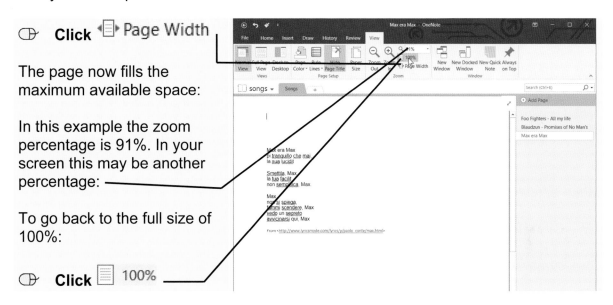

☞ **Click** ◄⬜► Page Width

The page now fills the maximum available space:

In this example the zoom percentage is 91%. In your screen this may be another percentage: ──────

To go back to the full size of 100%:

☞ **Click** ⬜ 100% ───────

2.8 Page Templates

Up to now you have added pages without any layout. Page templates provide some predetermined formatting for the creation of a new page. There are several categories with multiple templates: Academic, Blank, Business, Decorative, Planners. The names of these categories already suggest the expected appearance of the template.

There are two types of templates: the first group just provides design, the second group offers design, structure and content. The categories Decorative and Empty only offer styling. The categories Academic and Business offer design, content and structure.

For example, a meeting report will already contain an 'Agenda, Participants and to Do' list and in Project overview you will find 'Project name, Company name, etcetera.' already formatted for you. In the next section, you will be working with both types of templates.

 Please note:

It is not possible to add a page template to an existing page. Of course you can still open a new page template and copy the contents of an existing page to the new page.

Create a new page using a page template:

⊕ **Click the** ⌐Insert⌐ **tab**

⊕ **Click**

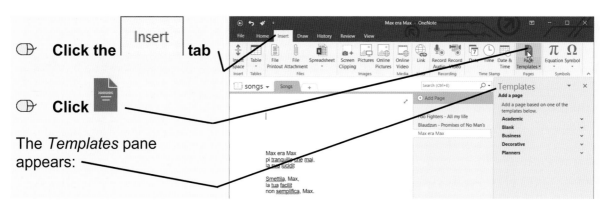

The *Templates* pane appears:

Make a new page with a decorative template:

⊕ **Click Decorative**

⊕ **Click Pushpins Corner**

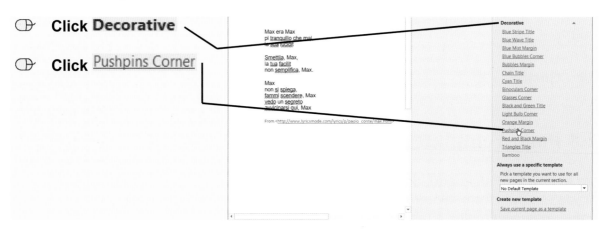

A new page appears Untitled page :

You see some formatting here, mostly in the upper left corner:

You can undo this new page and view another template:

⊕ **Click**

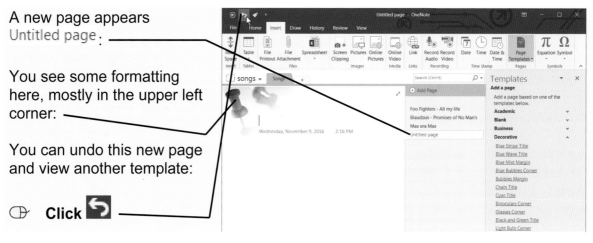

Make a new page with the Business template:

⊕ **Click Business**

⊕ **Click Simple Meeting Notes 2**

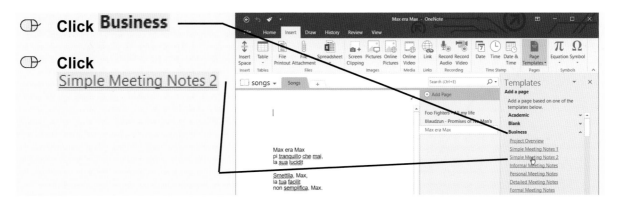

A new page appears: Meeting Title:

You see the formatting:

You can undo this new page and view another template:

⊕ **Click**

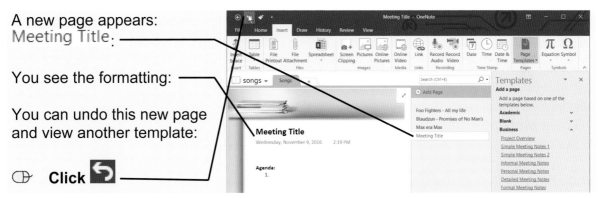

In the same way you can use the template Project Overview:

⊕ **Click Project Overview**

Naturally, the text in the example can be fully adjusted:

You can undo this new page:

⊕ **Click**

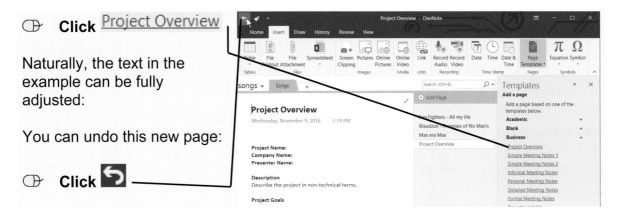

Some templates do not add color or graphics, but only contain a particular page size:

👆 **Click Blank**

👆 **Click A5**

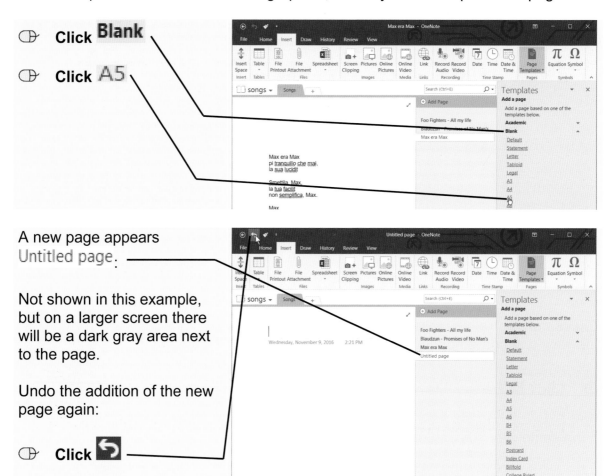

A new page appears
Untitled page.

Not shown in this example, but on a larger screen there will be a dark gray area next to the page.

Undo the addition of the new page again:

👆 **Click** ↩

You now have seen several options for formatting text and page layout in *OneNote*. In the following exercises, you can repeat these actions and take a look at some other templates.

👉 **Close the *Templates* pane** 🦶[14]

👉 **Close *OneNote*** 🦶[10]

2.9 Exercises

Have you forgotten how to perform a certain action? The number next to the footsteps tells you where to look it up at the end of the book in the appendix *How Do I Do That Again?*

Exercise 1: Cookbook

In this exercise you will make a cookbook in which you collect your favorite recipes.

☞ Open *OneNote*. ‿**1**

☞ Open the *Cookbook* notebook from the *Exercise files OneNote* folder. ‿**11**

☞ Zoom in to 110%. ‿**15**

☞ Open, if you wish, the page named *Pasta with 4 cheeses*. ‿**16**

☞ Apply Heading 2 on "Ingredients 4 persons" and "Preparation method". ‿**17**

☞ In the list of ingredients, adjust the name of each cheese to red and bold. ‿**18**

☞ Add task tags to all the ingredients and place a checkmark by the ingredients as shown below. 🐾**19**

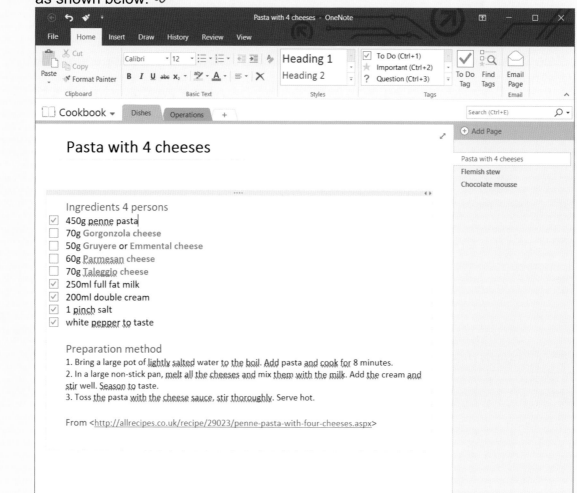

☞ Create a link from the word "pasta" to the page *Making pasta dough* in the section *Operations*. 🐾**20**

☞ Make the page color yellow. 🐾**21**

☞ Add rule lines (first option by the types of rule lines). 🐾**22**

This is the end result:

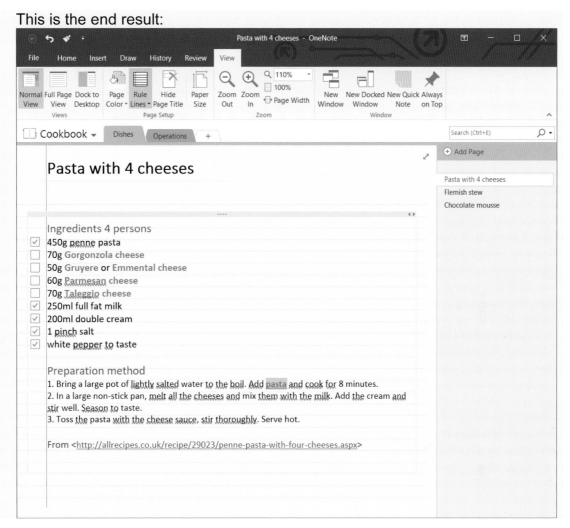

☞ Open the page *Flemish stew*. ⏃**16**

☞ Apply Heading 2 to "Ingredients 4 persons" and "Preparation method". ⏃**17**

☞ Add task tags to all ingredients and place a checkmark by "bay leaf", "salt" and "pepper". ⏃**19**

☞ Create a link from the words "pepper cake" to the page *Making pepper cake* in the section *Operations*. ⏃**20**

☞ Make the page yellow. ⏃**21**

☞ Add rule lines (first option by the types of rule lines). ⏃**22**

☞ Search for *Tag name* and make sure you now have a good overview of all the ingredients that have not been checked off and which you now have to get from the store. 👣23

☞ Close the pane. 👣14

☞ Make a new page by using the decorative "Bubbles Margin" page template. 👣24

☞ Dock the page on the desktop. 👣25

☞ Open the website www.simplyrecipes.com 👣13 and choose a dish you like.

☞ Give the new page the title of the recipe. 👣5

☞ Type the list of ingredients on the new page, followed by the text for the preparation method. 👣9

☞ Close the Internet browser. 👣10

☞ Turn off docking so you see the Normal page view again. 👣27

☞ Close *OneNote*. 👣10

2.10 Background Information

Word list

Docking	Securing or pinning a window to the desktop.
Hyperlink	A link to another page.
Label	A keyword you give to a particular content.
Page layout	Formatting options that can only be applied to a full page.
Rule lines	Lines that facilitate reading. Similar to the lines in a paper notebook.
Template	A pre-made layout and design applied to a page.

Source: OneNote help function, Wikipedia

Wiki's

In *section 2.2 Creating links* you made a link similar to those made in, for instance, Wikipedia (www.wikipedia.com). These are known as wikis.

A wiki is a collection of hypertext documents. It is an application that allows various editors to work together on processing web documents. The term is derived from the Hawaiian wiki, meaning 'quick, fast, agile.'

Wikipedia is the best known wiki, but not the only one.

2.11 Tips

 Tip

Adding more labels

You can apply more than one label to an item. This way the item can be found with multiple searches:

Here the third item shows
multiple labels:

 Tip

Always start from a template

If you would rather not start with an empty page, you can set a template as the default:

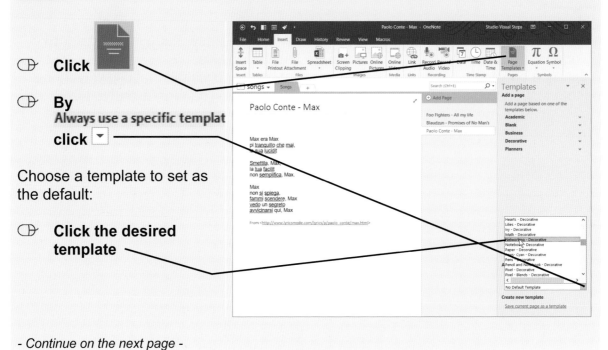

⊕ **Click**

⊕ **By**
Always use a specific templat
click ▼

Choose a template to set as
the default:

⊕ **Click the desired**
template

- Continue on the next page -

When you create a new
page, it will have the layout of
the selected template:

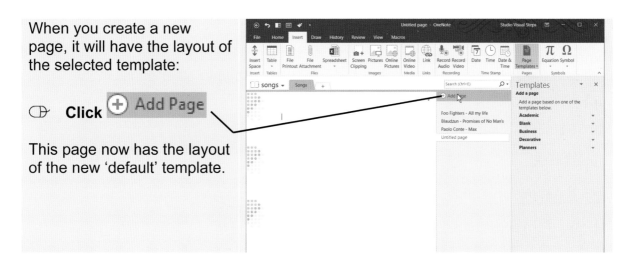

☞ **Click** ⊕ Add Page

This page now has the layout
of the new 'default' template.

💡 **Tip**

Spelling

OneNote has a built-in spellchecker. As a result, you will see a red zigzag line under
the relevant spelling errors. You can open the spellchecker as follows:

☞ **Click the** | Review | **tab**

☞ **Click** Spelling

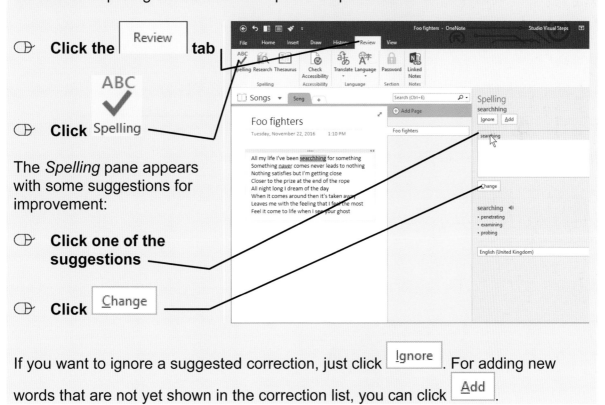

The *Spelling* pane appears
with some suggestions for
improvement:

☞ **Click one of the
suggestions**

☞ **Click** Change

If you want to ignore a suggested correction, just click Ignore . For adding new

words that are not yet shown in the correction list, you can click Add .

Tip

Hyperlinks to web pages

In this chapter you have learned how hyperlinks are made to other pages in the notebook. It is also possible to make hyperlinks to regular web pages:

☞ **Select the required text** 🦶12

⊕ **If necessary, click the** Insert **tab**

⊕ **Click** 🔗

⌨ **By** Address: **, type the desired web address**

⊕ **Click** OK

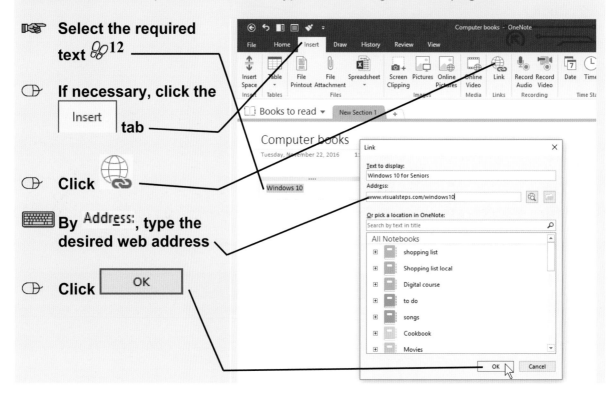

3. Inserting Files and Creating Links

In this chapter you will get started with creating a movie list and adding all kinds of media to it. First you will learn how to insert images that are stored on your computer, then you will search directly for images from within *OneNote* and add these as well.

Furthermore, you will learn how to change the stacking order of the images and rotate and mirror photographs. In addition, you will insert and attach documents and compare the differences between them.

You will also learn how to make screen shots, insert them, and copy text from the images. With a webcam or microphone at hand, you can also insert audio and video files. And finally, you will learn how to make calculations in *OneNote*.

In this chapter you will learn how to:

- copy content from websites and paste it in *OneNote*;
- insert images from your computer;
- delete images;
- insert online images;
- move and edit images;
- insert and link documents;
- make screen shots and insert them;
- convert text from images into editable text;
- record audio;
- record video;
- make calculations.

 Please note:

In order to work through the exercises in this chapter, you will need to use the practice files made for this book. You can download these files from the website accompanying the book **www.visualsteps.com/onenote2016**. In *Appendix B Download the exercise files* you can read how to do this.

3.1 Copy and Paste Text and Images from a Website in OneNote

The Internet is a source of information. It can be interesting to incorporate some online text or visual information into your notebook. This may be convenient if, for example, you want to collect your favorite recipes, plan a trip or make a list of your favorite movies. In this chapter you start by adding information about a movie from a website. You will be using an exercise file for this purpose:

☞ **Open *OneNote***

☞ **Open the *Movies* notebook from the *Exercise files OneNote* folder** ✍️**11**

You can see the notebook:

☞ **Make a new page called "Crash"** ✍️**6**

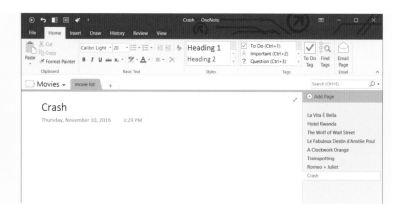

You will now look for information about a movie on the website. In this example the website www.imdb.com is used for this purpose. You will copy the text to the movies list in *OneNote*. First you will dock *OneNote* on the desktop and then open the website:

☞ **Dock *OneNote* on the desktop** ✍️**25**

👉 **Open the website**
www.imdb.com 🐾¹³

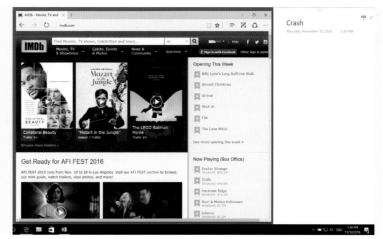

The website is on the left-hand side and *OneNote* on the right-hand side of the screen:

If you do not see this happen, you can place the browser on the left/hand side of the screen yourself.

You can search for the movie *Crash*:

In the search box:

⌨ **Type:** Crash

Some search results will appear:

👆 **Click**
Crash (2004)
Don Cheadle, Sandra Bullock

The webpage with information about the movie appears. Now you can copy some text:

👆 **Drag the scroll bar downwards**

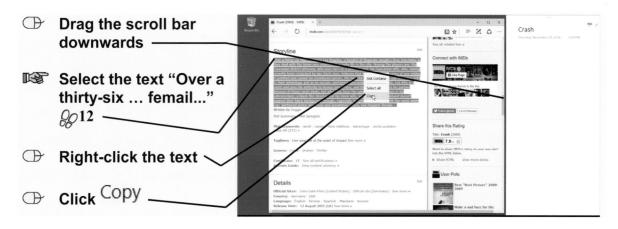

👉 **Select the text "Over a thirty-six … femail..."** 🐾¹²

👆 **Right-click the text**

👆 **Click** Copy

You can paste the text in *OneNote*:

In the window of *OneNote*:

👉 **Right-click an empty part below the title**

👉 **Click** 📋

The text is now in *OneNote*. You can return to the Normal display:

👉 **Click** ↗

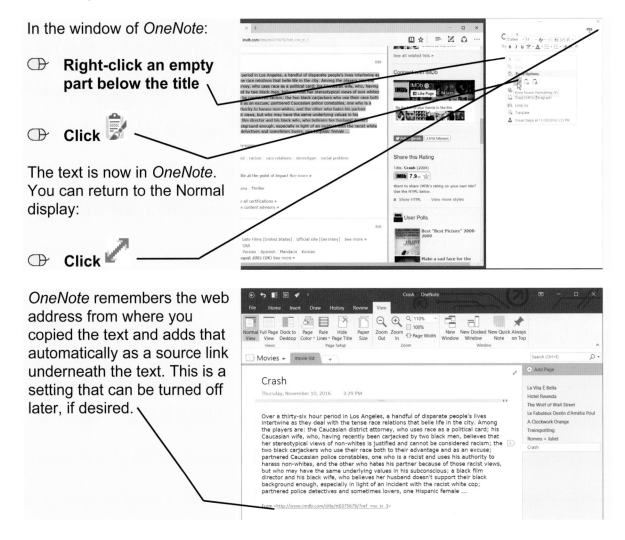

OneNote remembers the web address from where you copied the text and adds that automatically as a source link underneath the text. This is a setting that can be turned off later, if desired.

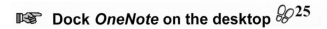

Now you can add an image as well. You can do this from the same website. Again you first have to dock *OneNote*:

👉 **Dock *OneNote* on the desktop** 👣²⁵

In the browser window you first delete the text selection:

⊕ **Click outside the selected text**

⊕ **Drag the scroll bar upwards** ⎯⎯⎯⎯⎯⎯

⊕ **Right-click the photo**

⊕ **Click** Copy

In the *OneNote* window you:

⊕ **Right-click below the text** ⎯⎯⎯

⊕ **Click**

The photo is now inserted in *OneNote* and you can return the Normal display:

⊕ **Click**

You see the result:

⊕ **If necessary, drag the scroll bar upwards**

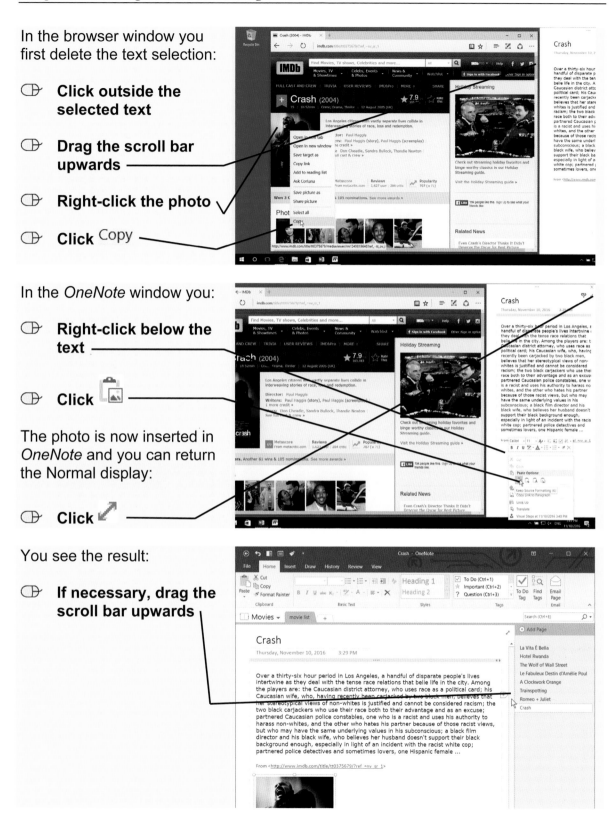

You can see that by copying text from websites you no longer have to rely solely on typing texts yourself. This way you can copy and combine a lot of interesting information from web pages.

 Close the window of the Internet browser ✂10

🐦 **Please note:**

Just like books, websites often feature copyrights. If you want to copy text and information from web pages and share this with others by print or digitally later on, it is advisable to ask for permission from the webmaster or owner of the website.

3.2 Inserting Images from Your Computer

It may be a cliché, but a picture is worth a thousand words. In this section you will learn how to insert images from your computer into your notes. First open the *Hotel Rwanda* page:

 Open the page *Hotel Rwanda* ✂16

You can now insert an image:

🖘 **Click anywhere to the right of the description text box**

🖘 **Click the** Insert **tab**

🖘 **Click** Pictures

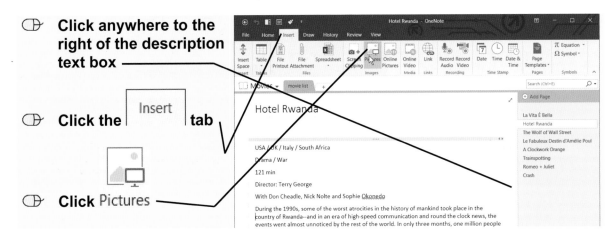

🐦 **Please note:**

Please be sure to click outside the text box. If you click inside the text box, the image would be placed on that spot.

You can find the image in the *Movies* folder in the *Exercise files OneNote* folder:

☞ **Open the *Movies*
   folder in the *Exercise
   files* folder** **11**

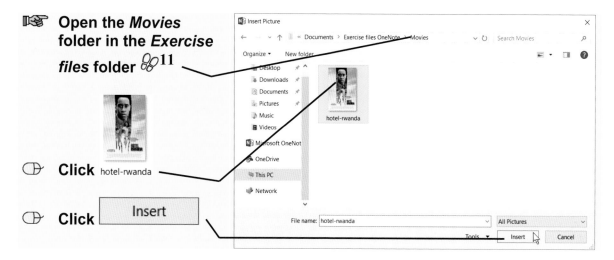

🖱 **Click** hotel-rwanda

🖱 **Click** ⬚ Insert

The image appears in your notebook right where you placed your cursor.

💡 **Tip**

Storing photos from a website
You just added a photo from your computer. If later on you would like to add a picture from a website, you can of course copy one from a website and paste it into *OneNote*. Just remember, that the options for editing are then limited.
In such a case, you may want to save the image from the website onto your computer. In the *Tips* at the end of this chapter, we explain how to do this.

3.3 Deleting a Picture/an Image

You can delete an image you no longer need:

🖱 **Click the image**

Around the image a dotted line appears. This indicates that the picture is selected:

⌨ **Click** ▢ Delete

The image is now gone.

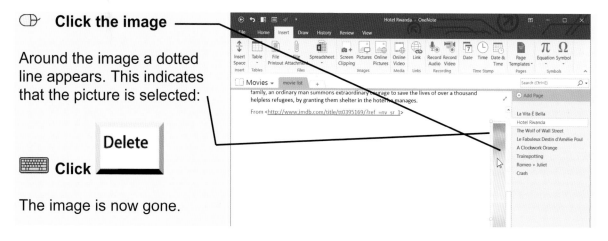

In this case you will keep the
image a while longer. You
can undo the procedure:

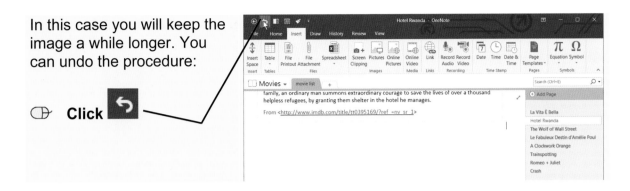

☞ **Click** ↩

3.4 Inserting an Image with Online Images

There is yet another way to insert images. It is also possible to search for images
directly from *OneNote*, and subsequently insert an image of your choice. In addition,
OneNote makes use of the *Bing* search engine. Here is how you do this:

☞ **If necessary, drag the
    scroll bar to the left**

☞ **Click in the middle
    below the description
    text box** ——

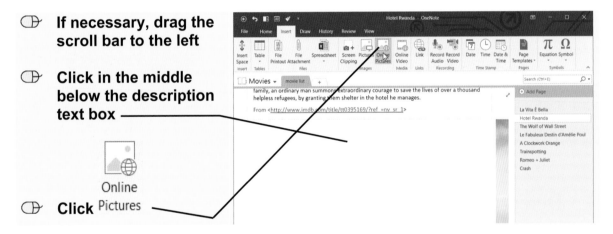

☞ **Click** Online Pictures

A window appears in which you can search for an image:

⌨ **Type:** Hotel Rwanda

⌨ **Press** Enter

It is also possible to insert
photos directly from
OneDrive, *Facebook* and
Flickr, but you do not need do
that now:

You now see the search results and can choose an image:

⊕ **Click an image** ——

⊕ **Click** [Insert]

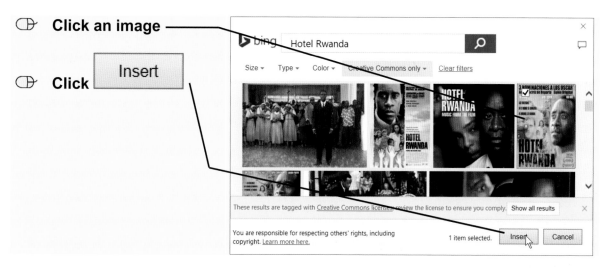

The image is placed below the text:

⊕ **If necessary, drag the scroll bar until it looks like this and you can see a part of both images**

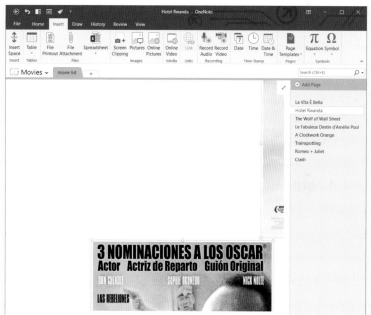

3.5 Moving and Editing Images

You can continue working with images by reducing, moving, rotating and mirroring the image. Later, you will learn how to position an image in front or behind another image. First we will show you how to reduce the size of an image:

To select an image:

☞ **If necessary, click the image** ────────

A dotted line appears around the image, indicating that the image is selected:

☞ **Place the pointer on the corner of the image** ────

The pointer changes to ↖↘:

☞ **Drag the corner towards the middle**

☞ **If necessary, drag the scroll bar downwards**

The image is now reduced:

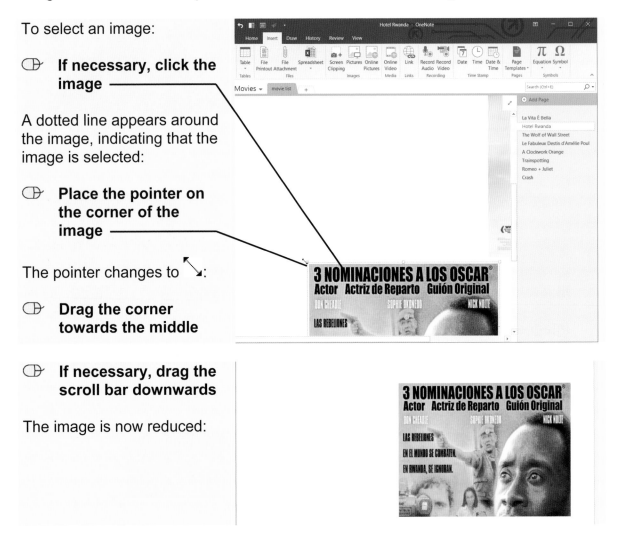

You can move the image and position it partly over another image.

For a better view of the whole page:

☞ **Zoom out until you have both images in view** 🐾**15**

👆 **If necessary, click the image**

👆 **Place the pointer on the image**

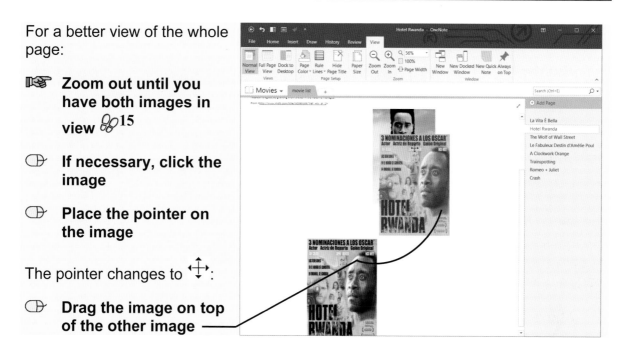

The pointer changes to ✛:

👆 **Drag the image on top of the other image** ——

Notice that the image is moved on top of the other image. You can now try placing it to the back or behind the other image:

👆 **Right-click the image**

👆 **Place the pointer on** Order ——

👆 **Click**
  ☐ Send Backward

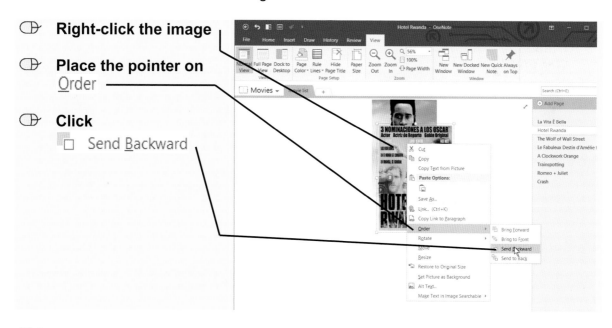

🕊 **Please note:**

Placing a picture on top of another, or moving them to the front or the back, is not possible if the images have been placed in a text box.

You can also rotate or mirror the image:

☞ **Right-click the image**

☞ **Place the pointer on**
   Rotate

☞ **Click**
   ◿ Rotate Right 90°

The image has been rotated.

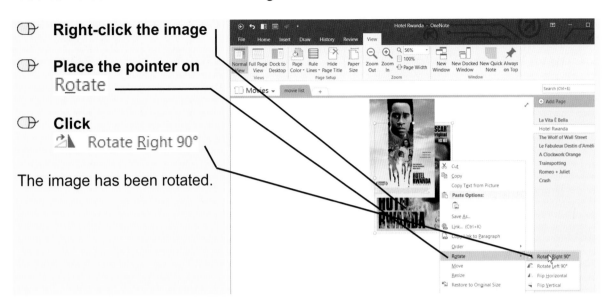

In a similar way you can mirror an image:

☞ **Click the other image**

☞ **Place the pointer on**
   Rotate

☞ **Click**
   ◣◢ Flip Horizontal

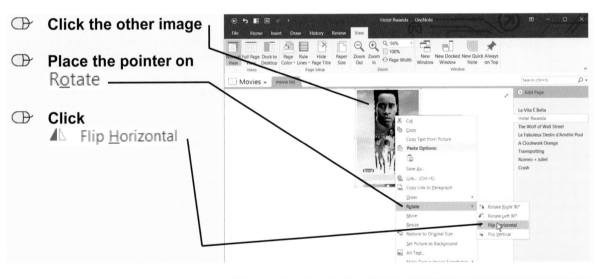

The image is now mirrored:

The text is also reversed. But you can leave it like this for the moment.

Please note:

In *OneNote* you cannot crop images. However, the use of *OneNote* in combination with the *OneTastic* app (see *section 7.2 OneTastic*) does offer this option. Of course it is also possible to crop your image to the correct size in advance by using a photo editing program.

3.6 Insering and Attaching Documents

You can insert and attach other files such as a *Word* or *Excel* document into your notes. Inserting means that you place a copy of the file into your notebook.

☞ **Open the page** *The Wolf of Wall Street* 🐾^{16}

☞ **Zoom in to page width** 🐾^{28}

👉 **Click the** │ Insert │ **tab**

👉 **Click below the text in the text box** ——

👉 **Click** 📎

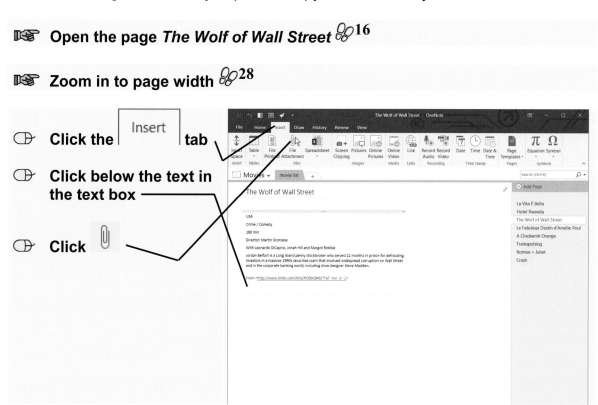

Browse to the folder that contains the *Word* document you want to insert. In this example the desired page can be found in the *Movies* folder in the *Exercise files OneNote* folder:

☞ **If necessary, open the Movies folder in the Exercise files OneNote folder** ✂11

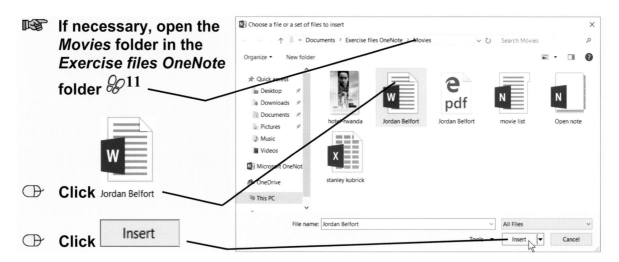

⊕ **Click** Jordan Belfort

⊕ **Click** Insert

You are offered a choice of either attaching the file or inserting it as a printout. To attach the file:

⊕ **Click** [icon] **Attach File**

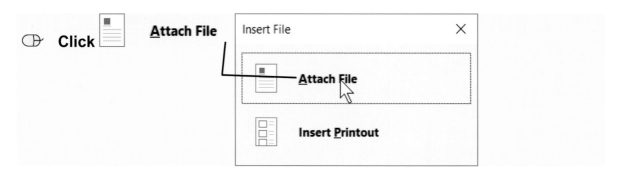

The icon of a *Word* document appears below the already existing text:

By holding the pointer on the icon, the file information appears:

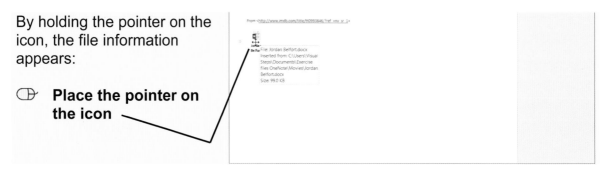

⊕ **Place the pointer on the icon**

You can now open and view the file:

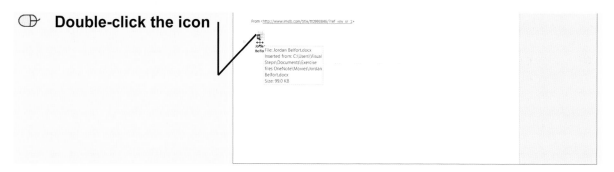

Double-click the icon

A notice appears reporting that the file is potentially harmful for your computer. In this example this is of course not the case:

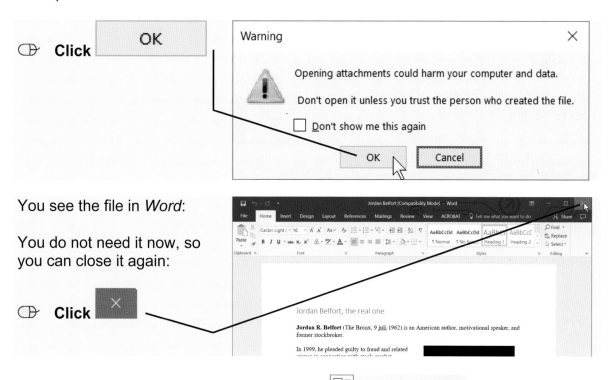

Click OK

You see the file in *Word*:

You do not need it now, so you can close it again:

Click ✕

You insert the file again, but now you choose ▤ **Insert Printout**:

☞ **Insert the file again below the first file**

⊕ **Click**

Insert Printout

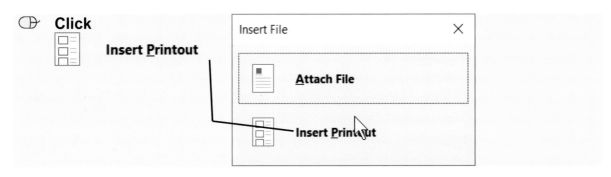

Inserting a file as a printout places an image of the *Word* document under the existing text. The printout acts like an inserted image but its text cannot be edited:

Next to this you see Jordan Belfort. If you double-click this, a file is opened in *Word*:

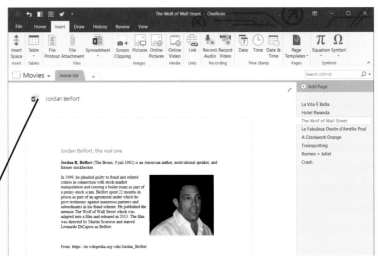

🔍 Tip
Using the Print File button

The ribbon shows the button Printout. This button lets you add a printout of a file very quickly.

You can now delete the added files:

⊕ **Click the file**

⌨ **Press** Delete

👉 **Follow the same procedure with the other two components**

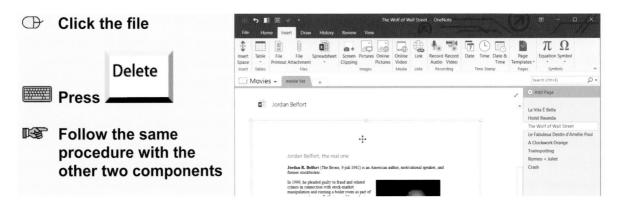

You can also attach an *Excel* document, embed an image of the spreadsheet or create a new *Excel* document in your notebook. This is done via a separate button. To insert a new *Excel* document:

☞ **If necessary, click below the text**

☞ **Click the** Insert **tab**

☞ **Click**

☞ **Click** New Excel Spreadsheet

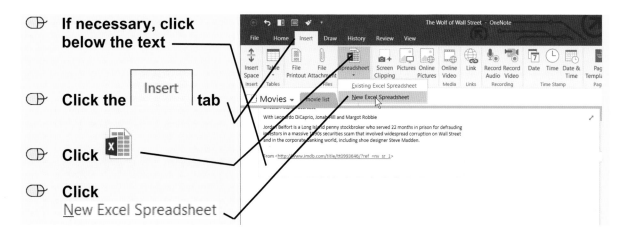

A new sheet appears:

In this new worksheet you can enter some data:

☞ **Click** ✏ Edit

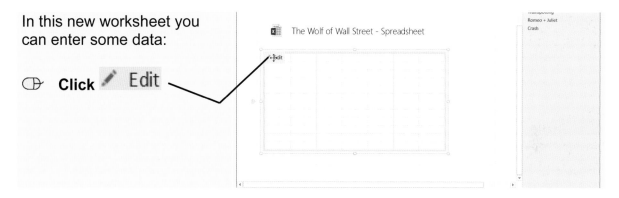

Microsoft Excel is opened and you can now type the data:

⌨ **Type several months**

⌨ **Type some numbers**

You close *Excel*:

☞ **Click** ✖

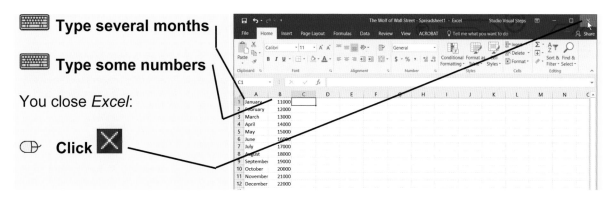

You now save the worksheet:

⊕ **Click**   Save

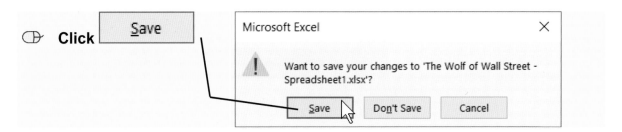

The data you filled in just now has been entered in the *OneNote* document as well:

You see the data in the table:

You also see a link to the file that you can edit as well after double-clicking it: ——

You can now delete this worksheet:

⊕ **Click the worksheet**

⌨ **Press**   Delete

☞ **Do the same with the *Word* component** ——

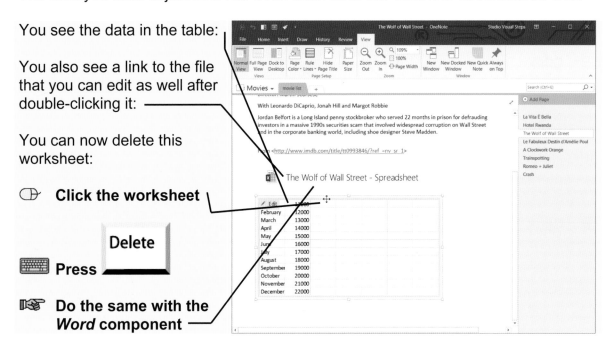

It is also possible to attach an already existing *Excel* document. You can do this on the page *A Clockwork Orange*.

☞ **Go the page *A Clockwork Orange*** 𝕮𝕽16

☞ **Zoom in to page width** 𝕮𝕽28

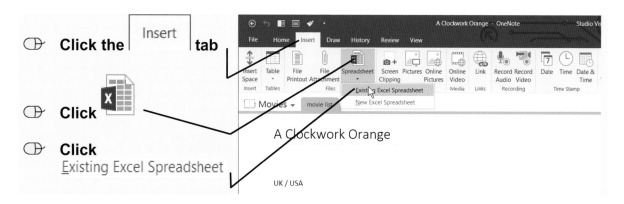

Click the Insert tab

Click

Click
Existing Excel Spreadsheet

You browse to the *Excel* document you want to attach:

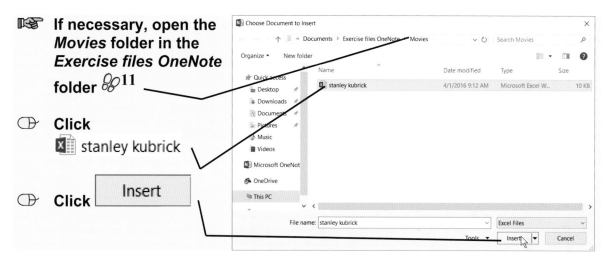

☞ **If necessary, open the Movies folder in the Exercise files OneNote folder** ✂11

Click
stanley kubrick

Click Insert

You now can choose the option to attach a file:

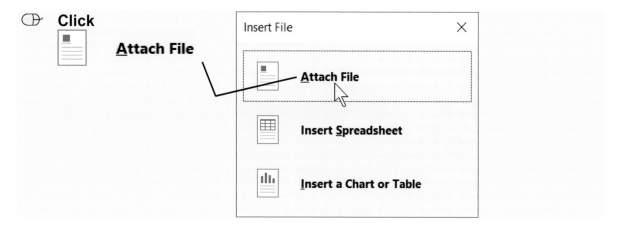

Click
Attach File

Below the text an icon of the *Excel* document appears:

☞ **Place the pointer on**

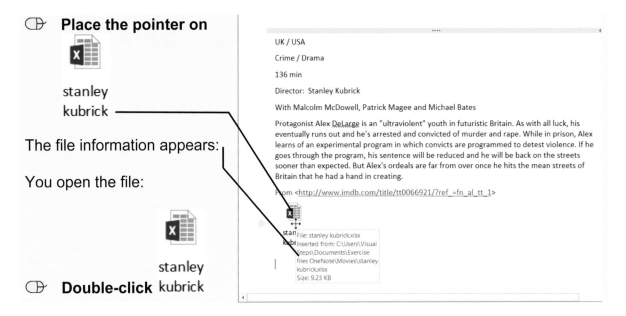

The file information appears:

You open the file:

☞ **Double-click**

A notice appears below, reporting that this file is potentially harmful for your computer. That is not the case for this file:

☞ **Click** OK

You see the *Excel* window with the document:

You can close the *Excel* window:

☞ **Click** ✕

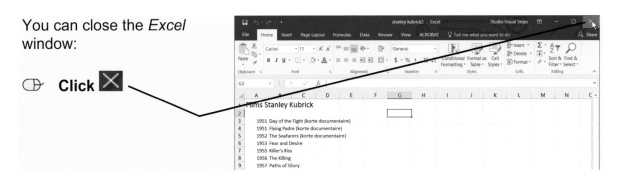

Now you try inserting an *Excel* file and see how it is displayed in *OneNote*. First you delete the current *Excel* file by undoing the last procedure:

☞ **Undo the last procedure** 🐾**29**

⊕ **Click**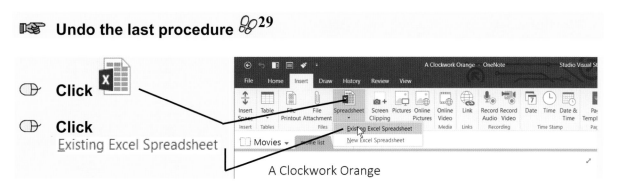

⊕ **Click**
  Existing Excel Spreadsheet

You browse to the *Excel* document you want to insert:

☞ **If necessary, open the**
  ***Movies* folder in the**
  Exercise files OneNote
  folder 🐾**11**

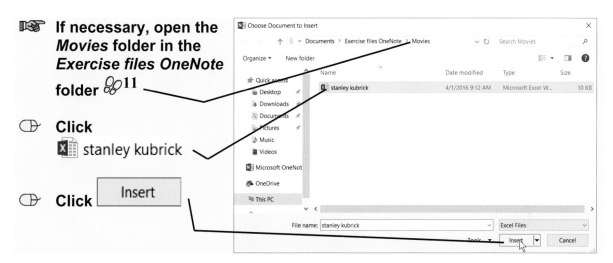

⊕ **Click**
  🅧 stanley kubrick

⊕ **Click** [Insert]

You can choose to attach or insert the file or insert a chart or table:

⊕ **Click**
  Insert Spreadsheet

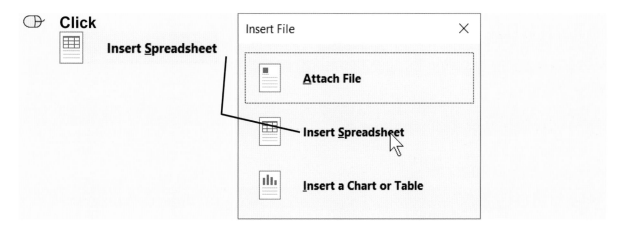

Below the text an icon of the *Excel* document appears as well as a static image of the spreadsheet. This static image has the properties as a regular image:

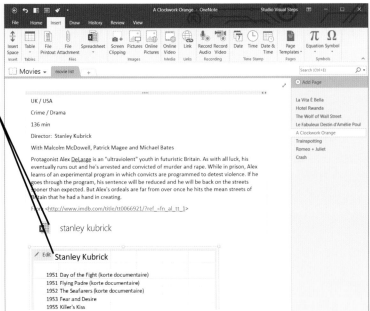

You can only start editing this document if you again click ✏ Edit or

 stanley kubrick.

 Please note:

Just remember, this is only a copy of your original *Excel* spreadsheet. Changes you make to the copy in *OneNote* will not show up in your original. And changing the original will not update the copy. The copy is simply a snapshot of what the spreadsheet looked like when you inserted it.

3.7 Making and Inserting Screen Shots

A screen shot, also known as screen print, is a printout of what is displayed on the computer screen at a certain time. The keyboard of a *Windows*-based computer by default already contains the key **PrtScn**. *OneNote* even goes a step further and includes a separate button for selecting which part of the screen you want to capture:

☞ **Go to the page *Trainspotting* ✔16**

☞ **Zoom in to 100% ✔15**

Before you can make a screen shot, you first must open the window you want to take a print from:

☞ **Open the website www.imdb.com** ✂️**13 and search for 'Trainspotting'**

☞ **Make sure *OneNote* is in the foreground again** ✂️**30**

You see the notebook:

Click the | Insert | **tab**

Click below the text in the text box ⎯

Click Clipping ⎯

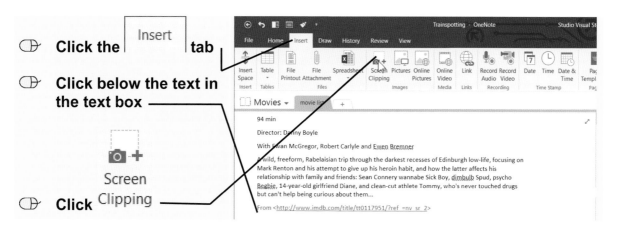

OneNote disappears and the previous screen appears with the Internet browser and the website www.imdb.com. A transparent gray surface covers the screen.

The pointer changes to ✛:

You can drag the pointer over the screen and select which part you want to print:

Drag the pointer over the area you want to capture ⎯

As soon as you release the mouse button, the screen shot of the selected area appears automatically in *OneNote*:

You see the screen shot in *OneNote* right on the spot where you had placed the cursor:

3.8 Converting Text from Images to Editable Text

OneNote also has a very nice option for removing text from images. You can test this technique by making a screen shot and then convert its texts into editable text.

☞ **Make a new page called *Invictus* ⠿⁶**

☞ **Make sure the website www.imdb.com comes to the foreground ⠿³⁰ and search for 'Invictus'**

☞ **Make a screen shot of the description and photograph of the film ⠿³¹**

The screen shot is now inserted. You now copy the text from the image:

👆 **Right-click the image**

👆 **Click**
   Copy Text from Picture

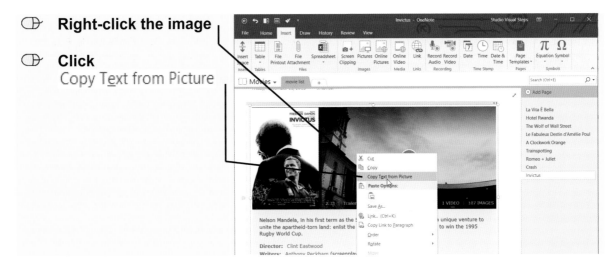

You paste the text from the image below the current image:

⊕ **Click below the image**

⌨ **Press simultaneously**

| Ctrl | and | V |

You now see the text: ─────

You may notice a few errors in the text. This can happen depending on the font and clarity of the text.

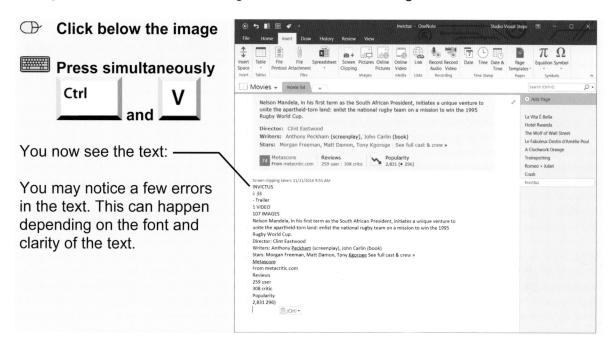

In *section 7.1 Office Lens* you will learn more about the handy *Office Lens* app. This app lets you create pictures from a book cover or a receipt, for instance. You can convert text into editable text and save the image in *OneNote*.

☞ **Close the Internet browser window** 10

3.9 Recording Audio

OneNote allows you to record audio. You do this using a microphone. Luckily today many laptops already have built-in microphones. And desktop computers can easily and relatively inexpensively be extended with an external microphone. Often webcams too have a built-in microphone. Even if you do not have a webcam or microphone, you can still read through this section.

☞ **Go to the page *Crash*** 16

You will now insert an audio fragment. After including the audio, an icon symbolizing the audio clip will appear:

 Click on the right-hand side of the text box

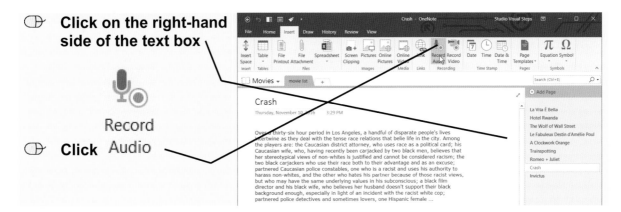

 Click Record Audio

🖐 **Please note:**
Make sure that you click outside of the text box, otherwise the icon will move to that text box as well.

An audio icon appears and in the ribbon you will notice a new *Record* tab. You can

start speaking from the moment you see Crash :

👉 **Speak a random text**

You can see how long the spoken text is

`00:13/00:13` :

For pausing the recording, you click ▐▐ :

In this case you can stop the recording immediately:

 Click

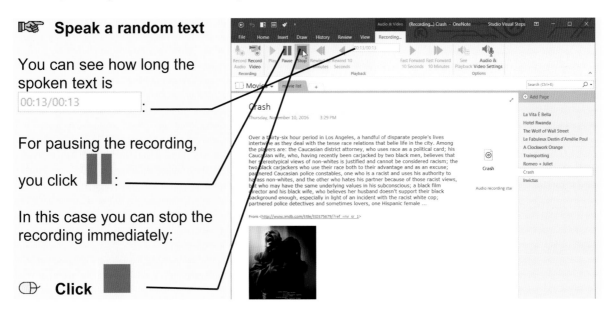

You can listen to the audio clip with your spoken text. Make sure that the sound of your computer or speakers is turned on:

For selecting the recording:

Click Crash

Click ▶

You now hear the text.

To stop the audio clip:

Click ■

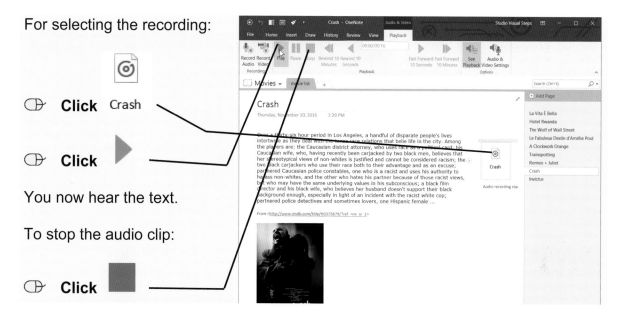

You can remove the clip now:

First select the file:

Click the edge of the text box

Press Delete

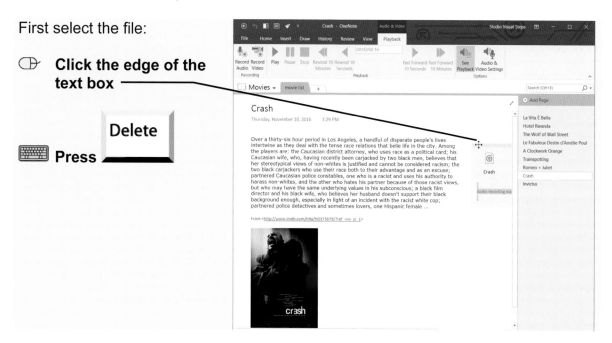

The icon disappears and the audio clip is deleted as well.

OneNote provides another interesting feature. While recording audio, *OneNote* can also register your actions. This can be the typing of text, applying some text formatting, inserting images, and so on. Take a look at how this works:

☞ **Click outside of the text box**

☞ **Click Record Audio**

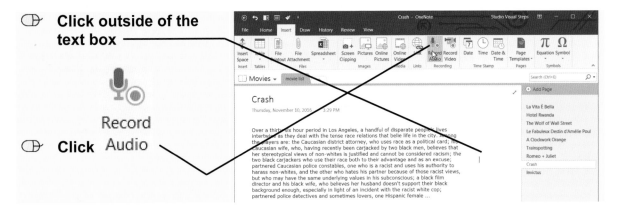

Now type a text and give it a color. You can try doing these things while simultaneously recording a spoken text:

☞ **Speak any text**

⌨ **Type above the text box:** Crash is a movie

☞ **Mark the text 'Crash is a movie' in red** ✂18

☞ **Click the Recording... tab**

☞ **Click** ▮

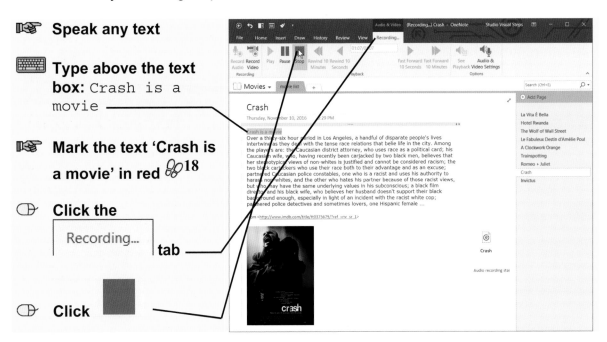

You can play the audio clip again and this time notice that your actions have been marked.

The 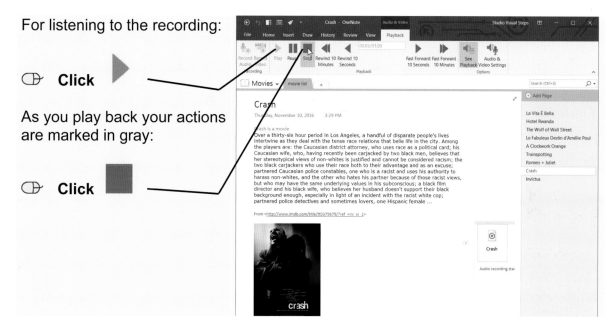 button on the right-hand side of the *Playback* tab must be shaded dark gray to play back the recorded actions.

For listening to the recording:

🖰 **Click** ▶

As you play back your actions are marked in gray:

🖰 **Click** ⬛

If multiple microphones or webcams are connected to your computer, you can select which of the audio and video settings you prefer:

🖰 **Click** Audio & Video Settings

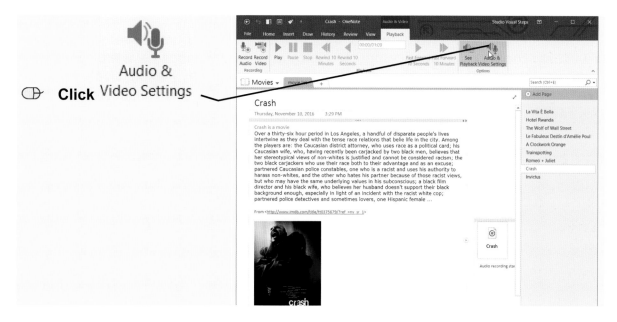

A new window opens:

Here you choose which
device to use for the audio
recording (microphone):

Choose which device to use
for the video recording
(webcam):

In this case you do not have
to change anything:

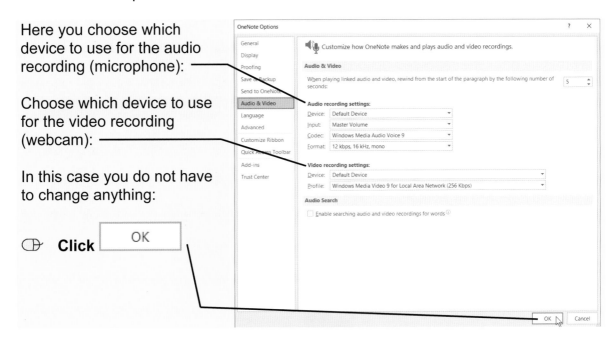

☞ **Click** [OK]

If you have a microphone, you have seen how easy it is to add audio to your
notebook. Your actions are recorded with it and can be displayed simultaneously
while the audio is playing.

3.10 Recording Video

In addition to audio, *OneNote* can also record video. It is of course essential to have
a webcam connected to your computer. Nowadays, most laptops have a built-in
webcam, but also desktop computers can easily and relatively inexpensively be
extended with an external webcam. If you have no webcam, you can just read or skip
this section.

You now will learn how to insert video. When you insert a video an icon will appear symbolizing the video clip:

☞ **Go to the page *Romeo + Juliet* ⸜⸝16**

⊕ **Click the ⎹ Insert ⎹ tab**

⊕ **Click below the text box**

⊕ **Click 🎥 Record Video**

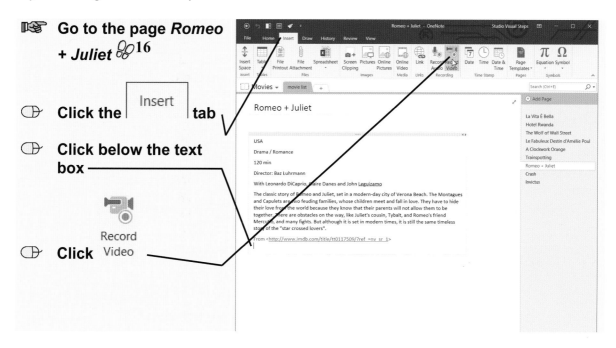

A video icon appears and you will see the new *Recording* tab. You can start recording:

As soon as the icon appears, you can start talking and a small video window will show you what is being recorded:

☞ **Speak a few words**

To pause the recording, click ⏸:

In this case you can stop the recording immediately:

⊕ **Click ⬛**

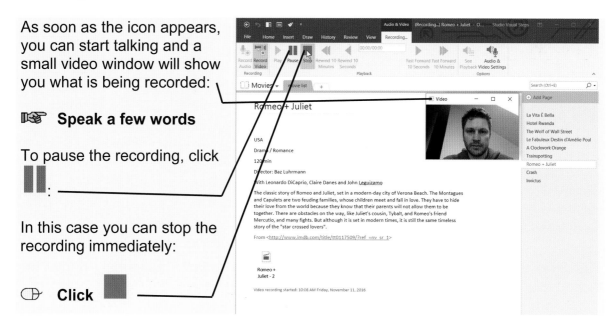

Now you can take a look at the video clip you just made:

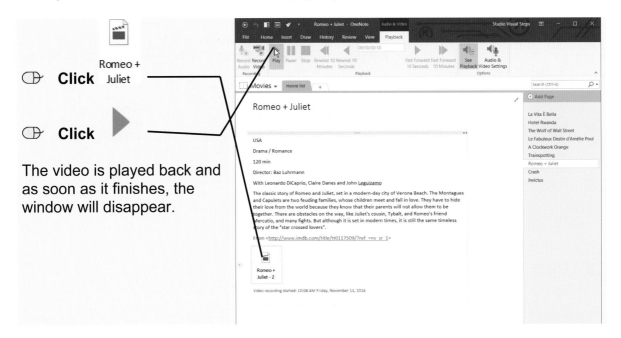

Click Romeo + Juliet

Click ▶

The video is played back and as soon as it finishes, the window will disappear.

You can delete the recording:

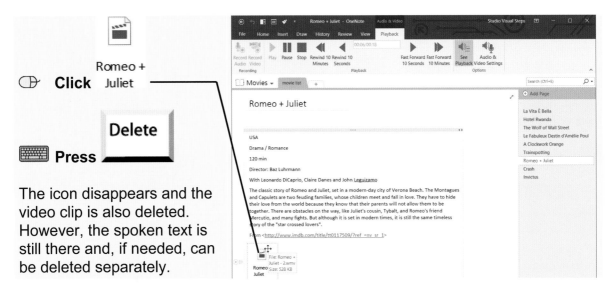

Click Romeo + Juliet

Press **Delete**

The icon disappears and the video clip is also deleted. However, the spoken text is still there and, if needed, can be deleted separately.

The video option does not offer the option of recording and simultaneously displaying these actions while the video is playing back.

3.11 Making Calculations

You can perform calculations in *OneNote*. The moment you close a sum, multiplication or other calculation with an '=' sign, you will see the result directly:

☞ **Go to the page *Le Fabuleux Destin d'Amélie Poulain* ᦰ¹⁶**

👉 **Click next to the text box**

⌨ **Type:** 199+299=

The moment you press the spacebar; you see the result:

⌨ **Press the spacebar**

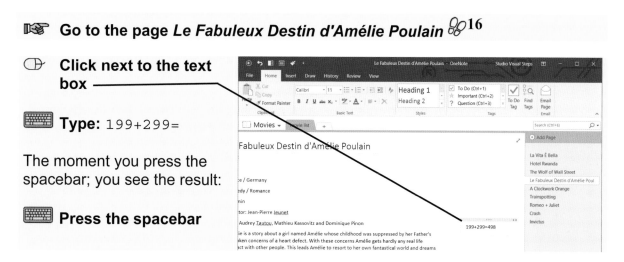

You can do other calculations, such as subtractions, multiplications and divisions in the same way.

☞ **Close *OneNote* ᦰ¹⁰**

In this chapter you have learned how to insert all kinds of media: images, screen shots, audio and video. You have also seen how easy it is to perform calculations in *OneNote*.

3.12 Exercises

Have you forgotten how to perform a certain action? The number next to the footsteps tells you where to look it up at the end of the book in the appendix *How Do I Do That Again*?

Exercise 1: Travel Diary

OneNote is an ideal program for collecting and compiling data. This can include a variety of different types of media: text, pictures, audio and video. In this exercise you will be creating a travel diary in *OneNote*.

☞ Open *OneNote*. ℘[1]

☞ Open the *Travel diary* notebook from the *Exercise files OneNote* folder. ℘[11]

You see the page *Days 1-3: London*.

☞ Open the website https://en.wikipedia.org/wiki/London ℘[13]

☞ Copy the text 'London (Engels: London) … London Assembly.' and paste it into the *OneNote* page. ℘[26]

☞ Go to the *Days 4-6: Paris* page. ℘[16]

☞ Open the website https://en.wikipedia.org/wiki/Louvre ℘[13]

☞ From the website, add a picture of the Louvre to the side of the text. ℘[33]

☞ Insert an online picture of the Eiffel Tower. ℘[34]

☞ Move the picture in such a way that it overlaps the Louvre picture. ℘[35]

☞ Change the stacking order and make sure the picture of the Eiffel Tower is now at the bottom. ℘[36]

☞ Go to the page *Days 7-9: Lisbon*. ℘[16]

On this page you will find a picture with some text included:

☞ Remove the text from the picture and paste this next to the image. ✂**37**

☞ Delete the image. ✂**38**

☞ Go to the section USA. ✂**39**

☞ Go to the *Days 10-14: New York City* page. ✂**16**

☞ Place the cursor above the existing text box. Record an audio clip, for instance of the text's first three sentences. ✂**40**

☞ Go to the *Days 15-16: Washington* page. ✂**16**

☞ Place the cursor above the existing text box. Record a video clip, for instance of the text's first three sentences. ✂**41**

☞ Go to the *Days 17-20: Seattle* page. ✂**16**

In the text box you will find all the distances of air travel:

☞ Calculate the total of all distances. ✂**42**

☞ Open the website http://www.hdwallpapers.in/walls/airplane_wing-wide.jpg ✂**13**

☞ Make a screen shot of the picture and add this to *OneNote*. ✂**31**

☞ Now place a printout of the file seattle.docx below it. ✂**43**

☞ Close *OneNote* and the Internet browser window. ✂**10**

3.13 Background Information

Glossary

Excel	*Microsoft* spreadsheet program which makes it possible to make calculations, keep lists, and a whole lot more. Just like *OneNote* it is a component of the *Microsoft Office* suite.
Facebook	Popular social medium.
Flickr	Online photo service for publishing your photos.
Stacking order	The order of images determining which image is on top and which is at the bottom.
Word	Microsoft's popular word processing program. *Word* is also a component of the *Microsoft Office* suite, just like *OneNote* is.

Source: OneNote help function, Wikipedia

3.14 Tips

 Tip

Saving pictures from a website
It is also possible to save a picture from a web page to your computer. From your computer, the image can then be inserted in *OneNote* as described in *section 3.2 Inserting images from your computer*.

▢⟶ **Right-click the image**

▢⟶ **Click**
Save picture as

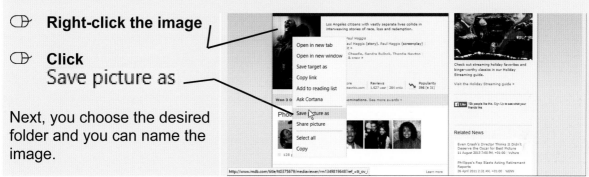

Next, you choose the desired folder and you can name the image.

 Tip

Inserting a PDF file
It is also possible to make a link to a PDF file:

▢⟶ **Click the** [Insert] **tab**

▢⟶ **Click outside the text box**

▢⟶ **Click** 📎

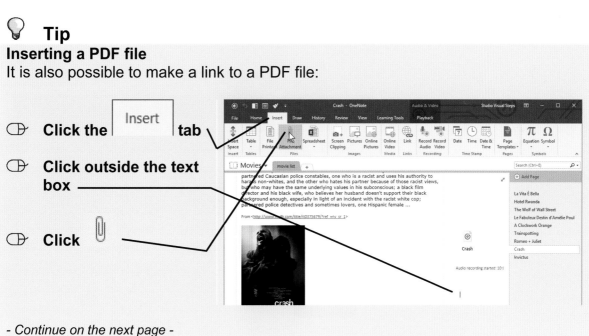

- Continue on the next page -

⊂⊅ **Click the desired file**

⊂⊅ **Click** Insert

⊂⊅ **Click**

      Attach File

You now see an icon for the
link to the PDF file:

You can also choose the
option for

      Insert Printout . In that
case an image of the file is
inserted instead.

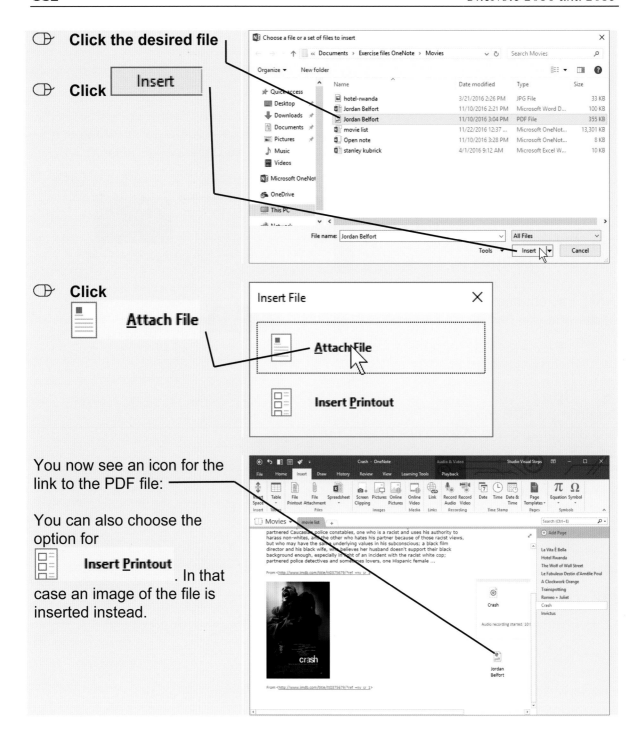

4. Digital Ink and the Search Function

In this chapter you will learn what digital ink is and how to draw or write in *OneNote*. This can be done using a special pen but you can also write and draw with the mouse. Drawing and writing with such a pen is also called doodling.

You will get acquainted with some of the features and benefits of digital ink. By working hands on with the digital pen you will quickly become aware of its value. Not only can you create notes and drawings with digital ink, you can also highlight sections of notes, use shapes and practice your handwriting technique.

Finally, you will learn how to use the search function to search through text, images and handwriting.

In this chapter you will:

- learn about the features and benefits of digital ink;
- how to draw with a digital pen or mouse;
- how to change the color and thickness of the ink;
- how to make selections;
- how to erase (wiping);
- how to insert shapes;
- how to convert handwriting into editable typed text;
- how to search through text, images and handwriting.

4.1 Digital Ink and the Digital Pen

Digital ink offers you the options of writing, drawing, sketching, coloring, highlighting, taking notes and much more. For many people writing is still done faster than typing. There are several ways to use digital ink. It can be done with your finger or mouse, but these options are not very accurate. The best option is to use a digital pen.

The digital pen converts words and drawings into digital data. The pen sends the 'ink' to the computer and stores it there. The digital pen is also known as a *stylus* or *active pen* (this is incidentally not a pointing pen with which you can scroll through a text on tablet and smartphone or can press buttons).

The active pen is a device that allows you to write directly on LCD screens. A touchpad like the *Wacom Bamboo*, is an alternative. Here you do not write directly on the screen, but on a separate touchpad. Both types of pens keep tabs on the pressure sensitivity: if you are tapping harder while drawing a line, a thicker line will appear.

In our opinion the *Microsoft Surface* with the extra accessory, the *Surface Pen,* works best. The *Surface* is a tablet device that in some ways acts like a regular PC. You can configure the *Surface Pen to* open *OneNote* directly by clicking the eraser button at the top of the pen.

If you do not have a digital pen, the mouse offers an alternative method. You can still follow the procedures in this chapter.

The *Surface Pen* (of the *Surface 3* and *4*):

In this chapter you can get started with an exercise file:

☞ **Open *OneNote*** ✂**1**

☞ **Open the *digital pen* notebook from the *Exercise files OneNote* folder** ℘11

You will see the pre-made *Draw* page.

If you own a digital pen, you can use it now. If you do not have a digital pen, just use your mouse (also called *finger*).

You will be using the options on the *Draw* tab:

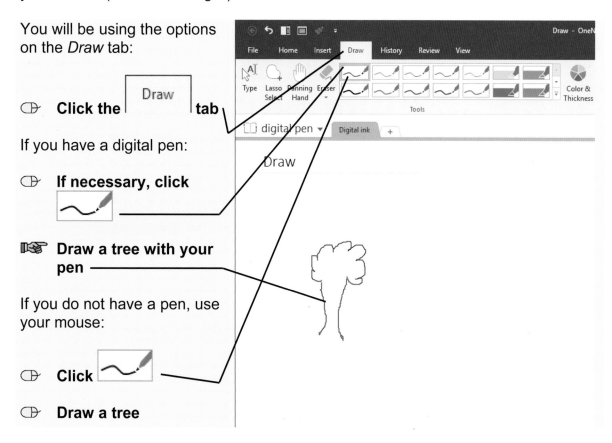

☞ **Click the** | Draw | **tab**

If you have a digital pen:

☞ **If necessary, click**

☞ **Draw a tree with your pen**

If you do not have a pen, use your mouse:

☞ **Click**

☞ **Draw a tree**

From now on this chapter makes no distinction between the pen and the mouse. If you have a digital pen, you can practice with that. If not, you can draw with your mouse.

4.2 Drawing: Color and Thickness

As you draw, you can choose from several options. It is important to know that there are two types of ink, or drawing styles:
• The pen for making notes;
• The marker with translucent ink and therefore ideal for highlighting an item.

On the *Draw* tab you can see right away some popular colors and thickness choices. Try now to draw a red flower with a green stem and leaves:

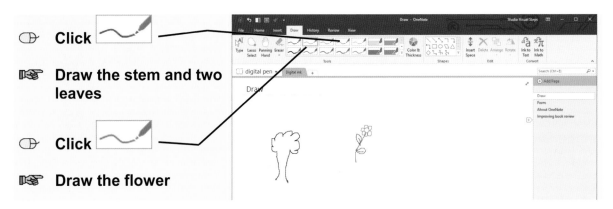

⊕ **Click**

☞ **Draw the stem and two leaves**

⊕ **Click**

☞ **Draw the flower**

You can also write with the pen. This is much easier to do with a pen than a mouse.

☞ **Go to the *Improving book review* page ✇16**

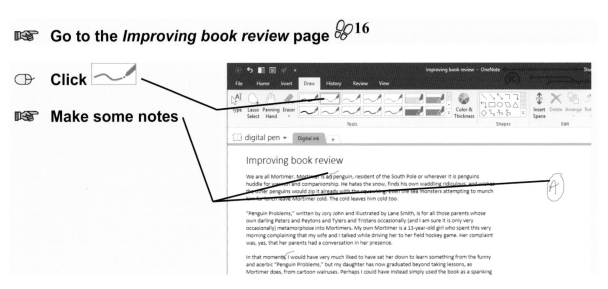

⊕ **Click**

☞ **Make some notes**

It is also possible to highlight with translucent ink, similar to a marker.

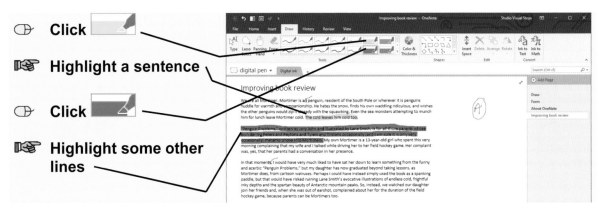

⊕ **Click**

☞ **Highlight a sentence**

⊕ **Click**

☞ **Highlight some other lines**

You can adjust the color and thickness manually:

☞ **Go to the *Draw* page**
✍16

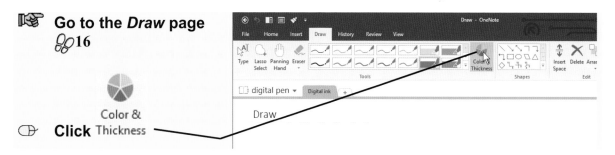

Color &
⊕ **Click** Thickness

Now a new window appears. Here you can select color and thickness. You can also select the use of a pen or highlighter:

In the example the pen is selected:

⊕ **Click a radio button** ⊚
by <u>P</u>en

Try using the third pen thickness and the color orange:

⊕ **Click** 〰

⊕ **Click** ▮

⊕ **Click** OK

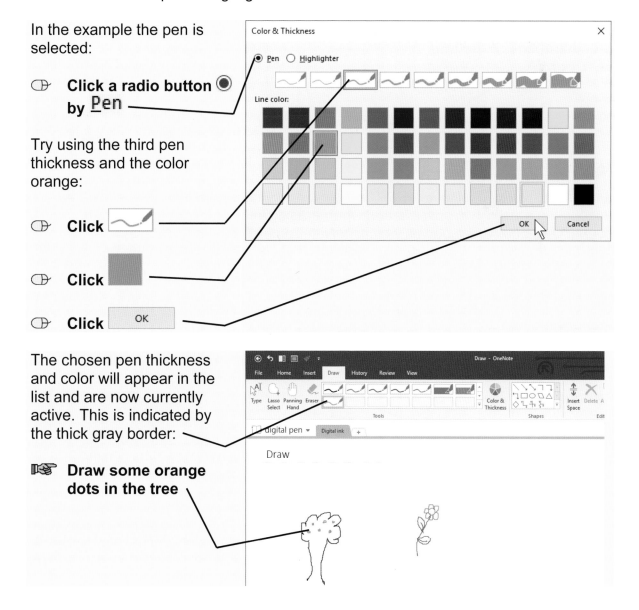

The chosen pen thickness and color will appear in the list and are now currently active. This is indicated by the thick gray border:

☞ **Draw some orange dots in the tree**

4.3 Drawing Selections and Erasing

Now that you have started drawing, you will probably want to be able to erase, move and reduce the size of your drawings. This is done by selecting and using the eraser. There are two types of erasers:

- the eraser which wipes parts that you drag over;
- the eraser that wipes pen strokes.

First you wipe a part of the drawing by using the pen stroke eraser:

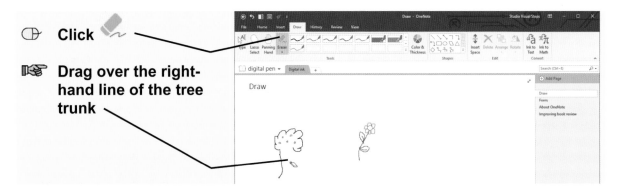

⊕ **Click**

☞ **Drag over the right-hand line of the tree trunk**

🖎 Please note:

It is difficult to see exactly what will be deleted and it takes a little practice getting used to the eraser. It is possible that when erasing lines of the same color the overlapping ones are wiped as well. *OneNote* remembers each line that is made with the pen and looks at these as separate. If you delete a line with the pen stroke eraser, it is usually a line that was drawn with one stroke before.

You now learn how to erase with a normal eraser. You can choose the size of the eraser yourself:

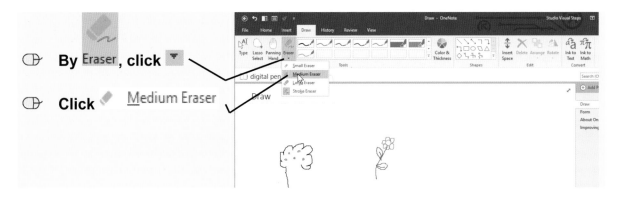

⊕ **By** Eraser **, click** ▼

⊕ **Click** Medium Eraser

☞ **Drag over the left line of the tree trunk** ——

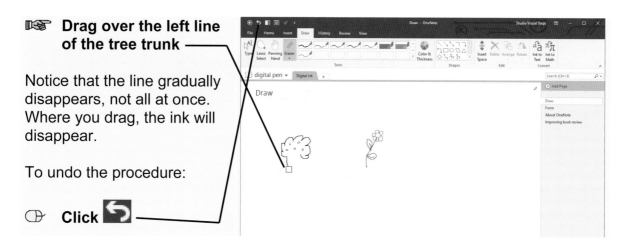

Notice that the line gradually disappears, not all at once. Where you drag, the ink will disappear.

To undo the procedure:

⊕ **Click** ↩ ——

Making selections is also an option in *OneNote*. This enables you to move, enlarge, reduce, erase or rotate elements of the drawing:

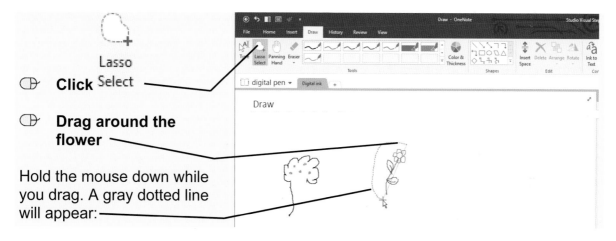

⊕ **Click** Select ——

⊕ **Drag around the flower** ——

Hold the mouse down while you drag. A gray dotted line will appear:——

Continue dragging further until you reach the point where you started:

⊕ **Drag around the flower from starting point to finish** ——

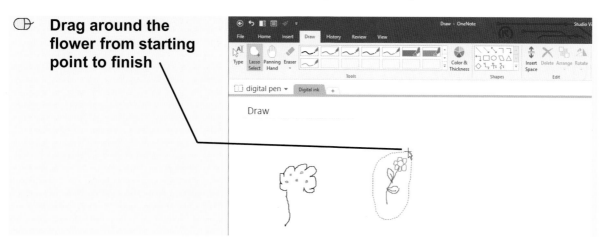

When you release the mouse button, the selection appears:

The flower is outlined by a thick gray line, and a dotted border with handles appears:

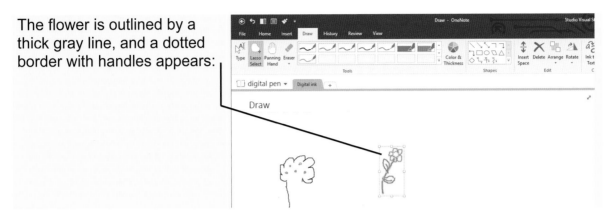

You can move the flower:

⊕ **Drag the flower to the left**

As you drag the pointer looks like this ✛:

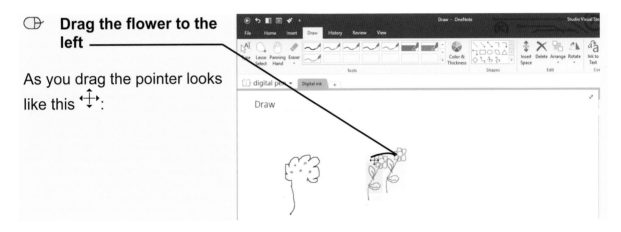

You can also enlarge or reduce the flower:

⊕ **Place the pointer in the upper right corner**

The pointer changes to ⤢ :

⊕ **Drag a little down to the left**

The image becomes smaller:

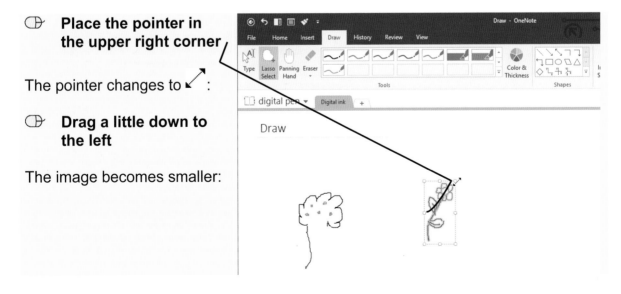

Please note:

When you enlarge an image, the detail of the elements may become less sharp.

 Tip

Other options in selecting

When a drawing is selected, you can delete it by pressing **Delete**. You can also rotate a selection. This is done the same way as rotating images. See *section 3.5 Moving and editing images*.

 Tip

Erasing with the digital pen

With the digital pen you can erase with the button on top. This works the same way as an ordinary pen.

While drawing you can switch back to the typing mode:

⊕ **Click** Type

You are now able to type, but you do not need to do that just yet.

You have practiced a bit with drawing, and have seen the options to reduce, enlarge, rotate and delete a drawing. You have also learned how to erase digital ink by using two types of erasers. Before switching back to typing mode you can take a look at some ot the shape options.

4.4 Inserting Shapes

OneNote contains different shapes and forms that are very easy to insert. Again you have a choice from different colors and thicknesses.

☞ **Go to the *Shapes* page** 16

Start by drawing an arrow:

First choose the desired color
and line thickness:

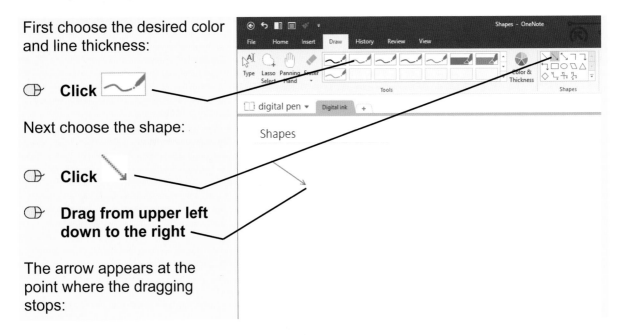

⊕ **Click** ✏️

Next choose the shape:

⊕ **Click** ↘️

⊕ **Drag from upper left
down to the right**

The arrow appears at the
point where the dragging
stops:

In the same manner you can draw other shapes:

👉 **Draw the shapes as
shown here**

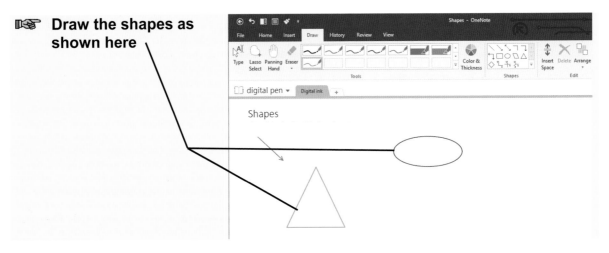

There are a number of shapes you have not seen yet:

⊕ **By** Shapes **, click** ▼

Draw a diagram:

⊕ **Click** Y X

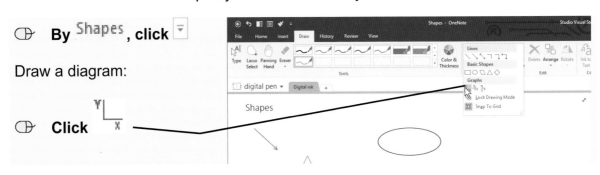

⊕ **Drag from the upper left to the right below**

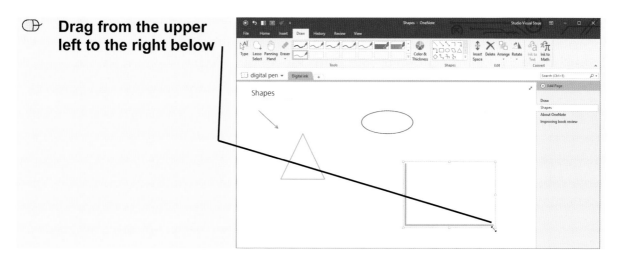

This type of diagram may be interesting if you quickly want to draw a graph.

You also have the option to display a grid while you are drawing. This way you can neatly align the shapes.

⊕ **By** Shapes **, click** ▾

Aligning to grid is active by default. You can turn this off:

⊕ **Click** Snap To Grid

If this button looks like this, it is active. If it looks like this it is inactive.

⊕ **Click** ◇

☞ **Draw the shape**

Note during the drawing that the shape no longer enlarges incrementally, but more gradually and smoothly.

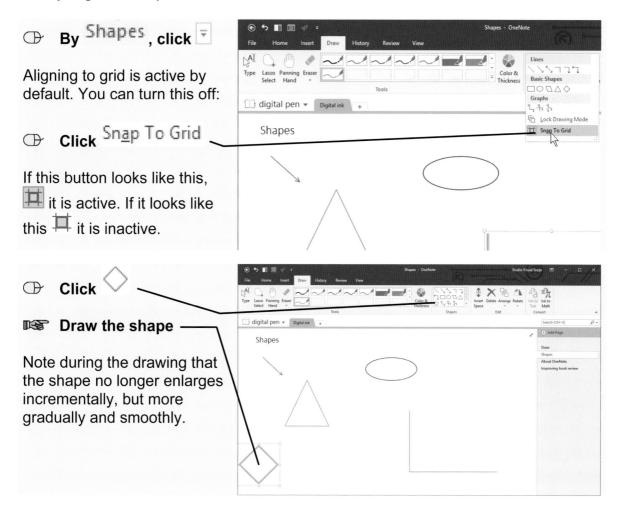

Shapes can be moved, enlarged, reduced, wiped and erased. Furthermore, it is possible to rotate, delete and arrange the shapes as desired. You can find all of these options in the *Edit* group on the *Draw* tab.

4.5 Converting Handwriting into Typed Text

By using digital ink, you can create or insert more than just drawings. You can also write with it. Interestingly, *OneNote* is able to recognize this handwriting and can even convert it into editable text. There is just one condition: your handwriting needs to be clear enough for *OneNote* to recognize it as written text.

☞ **Go to the *About OneNote* page** 🦶16

On this page handwritten text is already added. You now select this written text:

You convert the handwritten into typed text:

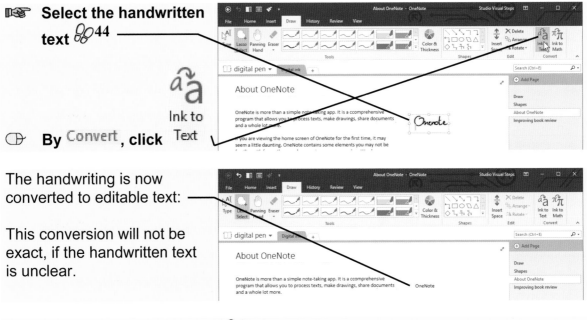

Select the handwritten text 🦶44

☞ **By Convert, click Ink to Text**

The handwriting is now converted to editable text:

This conversion will not be exact, if the handwritten text is unclear.

☞ **Undo the last procedure** 🦶29

You have learned to convert your handwriting into typed text. Although this is a very smart and useful feature, it's not always perfect in *OneNote*. Especially when using multiple words. The more you practice writing text in *OneNote* the better results you will get and *Microsoft* may also improve this function over time.

4.6 Searching

Another great feature in *OneNote* is its search function. This function does not search through typed text only, but also through handwriting and even images.

☞ **Go to *Improving book review* page ✂️16**

In the search box in the upper right corner you can search for a word in the typed text:

🖰 **Click the search box**

⌨️ **Type**: Mortime

The search results are shown immediately and the search term is highlighted in the text:

You can close the search pane:

🖰 **Click ✕**

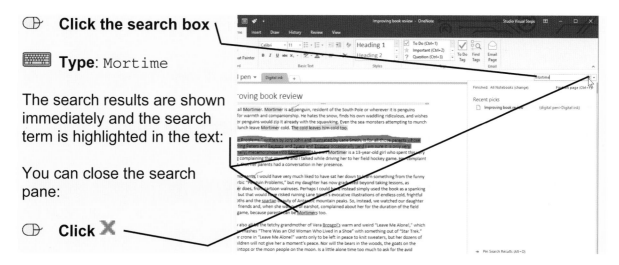

Now you can try a different search. Here the search term will be present in the handwriting, in an image and on several pages:

🖰 **Click the search box**

⌨️ **Type**: OneNote

Search results may be found in other notebooks:

🖰 **Click on the first search result on the About OneNote page**

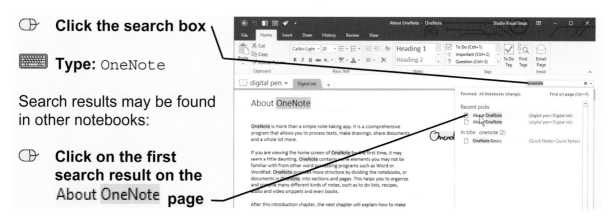

'*OneNote*' is found in the handwriting and in the image :

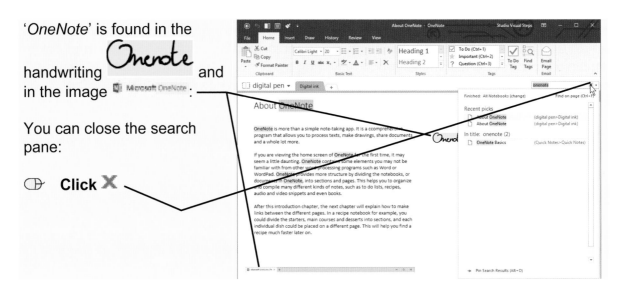

You can close the search pane:

☞ **Click ✕**

Notice that the word '*OneNote*' is now recognized in the notes, while the handwriting conversion failed in the previous section. Sometimes you need to indicate that the text in an image should be searchable. You can add a new image, indicating that the text is searchable:

☞ **Make a new page with the title *Australia* ⅋⁶**

☞ **Add the image named Australia.jpg from the *digital pen* subfolder in the *Exercises OneNote* folder ⅋³²**

☞ **Right-click the image**

☞ **Click**
Make Text in Image Searchable

☞ **Click**
English (United States)

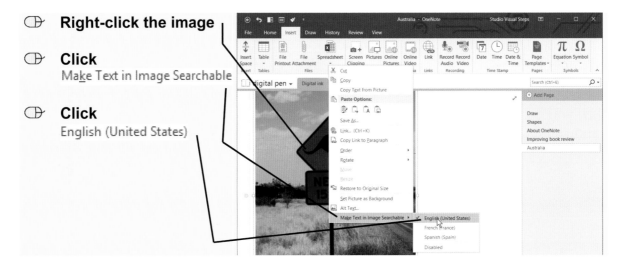

Now perform the search action:

⟐ **Click the search box**

⌨ **Type**: Next

'Next' is found in the picture and is highlighted:

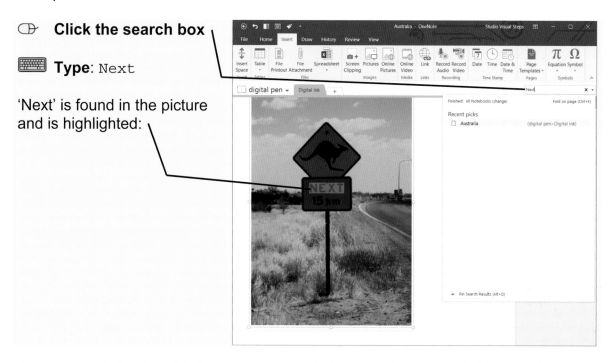

☞ **Close *OneNote* 👣10**

In this chapter, you have learned how to use digital ink for drawing, and how to insert shapes. You also used the search function and have seen that it can search through each notebook in your *OneDrive* account or on your PC. Search terms can be found not only in regular typed text, but also in images and handwritten text.

4.7 Exercises

The following exercises will help you master what you have just learned. Have you forgotten how to perform a certain action? The number next to the footsteps tells you where to look it up at the end of the book in the appendix *How Do I Do That Again*?

Exercise 1: Drawing and writing

A common request these days, is to complete and sign documents. It saves time if this can be done digitally. In this exercise, you see a form from a kinder class, which must be completed for ordering class photos. On the paper document a picture has been taken with *Office Lens* (see *section 7.1 Office Lens*) and inserted into *OneNote*.

☞ Open *OneNote* ᵇ𝓅**1**

☞ Make a new notebook and save it on *OneDrive* with the name *Class photo*. Do not share the document. ᵇ𝓅**2**

☞ Insert the image *Class photo*. ᵇ𝓅**32**

☞ Make the text in the image searchable. ᵇ𝓅**45**

☞ Search the word 'group' ᵇ𝓅**46** and highlight the word in blue. ᵇ𝓅**47**

☞ Now fill in the form with the digital pen or mouse and use the thin red ink. ✂**48**

Name: *Chris*

Group: *2nd*

Pay just $25 for ALL digital proofs on CD without imprinting. Images sold AS IS.
No color correction, crop or extra digital editing. No printing release form *
Resolution up to 500x700 DPI. Excellent quality for E-mails, I-Phones, TV screens

Write down AMC POSE PROOF NUMBER(s) or ATTACH AMC POSE PROOF(s).
You can use pictures from different years (up to 10 years available)

1st *Student(s) Name* ___Chris_____

Starting AMC Proof Number ___1___	*Last* AMC Proof Number ___1___	**$25**
2nd starting AMC Proof Number _____	*2nd last* AMC Proof Number _____	**$5**
3rd starting AMC Proof Number _____	*3rd last* AMC Proof Number _____	**$5**

For class picture on CD - ADD **$5** _____
                          Teacher Name   Class / Room

For each extra person please ADD **just $10** (SAME FAMILY ONLY)

2nd *Student(s) Name* _____

Starting AMC Proof Number _____	*Last* AMC Proof Number _____	**$10**
2nd starting AMC Proof Number _____	*2nd last* AMC Proof Number _____	**$5**
3rd starting AMC Proof Number _____	*3rd last* AMC Proof Number _____	**$5**

For class picture on CD - ADD **$5** _____
                          Teacher Name   Class / Room

☞ Place you signature below. ✂**48**

☞ Write down next to the signature in blue: `Payment included.` ✂**48**

2nd *Student(s) Name* _____

Starting AMC Proof Number _____	*Last* AMC Proof Number _____	**$10**
2nd starting AMC Proof Number _____	*2nd last* AMC Proof Number _____	**$5**
3rd starting AMC Proof Number _____	*3rd last* AMC Proof Number _____	**$5**

For class picture on CD - ADD **$5** _____
                          Teacher Name   Class / Room

TOTAL PAID FOR DIGITAL CD _____ Signature

Payment included

* If you need High Resolution image for prints up to 30"x60"
with printing release form - order single item Z.

☞ Select the blue handwritten text 'Payment included' $\mathcal{O}\!\mathcal{O}$**44** and convert it into editable text. $\mathcal{O}\!\mathcal{O}$**49**

☞ Make a new page and name this 'Color print'. $\mathcal{O}\!\mathcal{O}$**6**

☞ Insert the image named *Color print*. $\mathcal{O}\!\mathcal{O}$**32**

☞ Fill in the print with several colors. Use a pen width of 5 mm and the marker in such a way that the black lines will not be overlapped. $\mathcal{O}\!\mathcal{O}$**48**

Note that *OneNote* can be used in this digital way by children for coloring.

☞ Close *OneNote*. $\mathcal{O}\!\mathcal{O}$**10**

4.8 Background Information

Word list

Digital ink   Digital ink offers the option to write, draw, color, highlight, make notes and many things more.

Stylus   A pen for inputting commands to a graphics tablet (also known as a digitizer, drawing tablet, digital drawing tablet, pen tablet) or to a laptop or tablet's touchscreen. Also named *active pen*.

Surface Pen   A pen for inputting commands but with more features such as the ability to detect different levels pressure. Also has an eraser on the opposite end of the pen.

Touchpad   A touch-sensitive surface that can translate the motion and position of a user's fingers to a relative position on the operating system that is outputted to the screen of a computer, laptop or tablet.

Source: OneNote help function, Wikipedia

Planning and sketching of scenarios
Cartoonist Wim Swerts uses *OneNote* to plan and sketch scenarios. This is another example of how *OneNote* can be used.

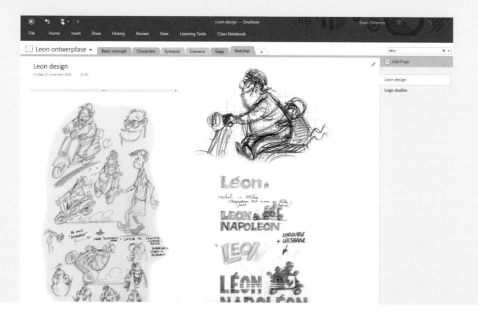

4.9 Tips

 Tip

Converting completely handwritten texts into typed texts
If no selection is made, *OneNote* will automatically convert the full written text on the active page into typed text:

☞ **Write down several words and/or sentences on one page** ✂⁴⁸

Please note: do not make a selection!

Ink to
⊕ **Click** Text

In just one try all text is converted into typed text.

5. Sharing Notebooks

In this chapter, you will learn more about the various versions that *OneNote* comes in. The full desktop application that is a part of the *Office* suite, a mobile app and a web app. You will learn how to share notebooks with others who in turn can view or even edit the notebook. You use version control to make sure that others cannot remove key information from a shared notebook.

In this chapter you will learn how to:

- explore the web app;
- explore the *Windows 10* desktop app;
- work with *OneNote* on a Mac computer;
- share a notebook that allows editing;
- work with version control;
- work with the trash can;
- secure sections.

5.1 A Summary of OneNote Apps and Versions

OneNote exists in different forms and versions. First, there is the distinction between the desktop program, the mobile app and the web app. The full desktop application is a part of the paid *Office* suite, for instance the 2016 and 2013 versions. This book uses the *OneNote* desktop version and the screen shots you see are from version 2016.

Next, there is the free web app. This is the online version of *OneNote* that requires sign in. The web app has fewer options and some features are omitted altogether.

There is also a free app for smartphones and tablets. This is available for *iOS* on the iPad and iPhone, for *Android* devices and for the *Windows* Phone. At the end of this chapter you will find more information about this app.

Finally, for *Windows* on the PC a separate free app is also available. *Windows 10* has this app installed by default. On a computer running *Windows 8.1* and *Windows 7,* the app can be downloaded for free from the *OneNote* website: www.onenote.com/download

In the following sections you will learn more about the different apps.

5.2 OneNote for Windows

The *OneNote* app comes preinstalled and is integrated into *Windows 10*. In *Windows 8.1* and *Windows 7* this is simply called *OneNote* (and this can give some confusion).

What is interesting about this app is that everyone with a *Windows* PC already has it (or can download it). It is also frequently updated with new features being added all the time. The distribution of these updates is done in waves, so it may be possible that you not have received the latest update while someone else you know already has.

In the next few examples, you will see screen shots and information for the built-in *OneNote* app in *Windows 10*. If you are using *Windows 8.1* or *Windows 7*, you may want to download *OneNote* first or just read through this section. Here we will focus primarily on the differences between the free built-in app on *Windows 10* and the desktop version of *OneNote 2016* or *2013* that is part of the *Office* suite.

Click [■]

Type: `onenote`

Click [NE] **OneNote**

Please note: if you see the text 'trusted *Windows Store* app', please click that version.

The app will now open. When you start *OneNote* for the first time, you will see a number of information windows:

Click [>] **twice**

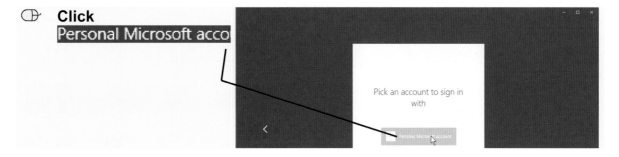

You must now choose how you want to login. In this example, use the *OneDrive* account that you also used at the beginning of *Chapter 1 Starting a new notebook*:

Click
Personal Microsoft acco|

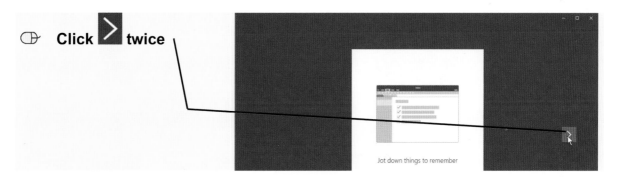

In the next window:

Type your email address and password

Click **Sign in**

If you are not yet registered in *Windows* with a *OneDrive* user account, you may see the following window. In this example, make sure you only login to the *OneNote* app and refrain from using the *OneDrive* user account:

☞ **Click**
   Sign in to just this app

The *OneNote* app is set up:

☞ **Click**
   Start using OneNote

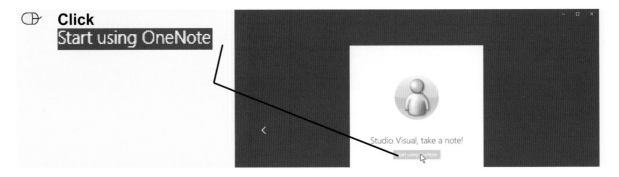

OneNote now connects to *OneDrive* and automatically retrieves the notebooks you have stored online. You will see that in the next window:

You may notice a certain similarity to *OneNote 2016* or *2013*, but there are noticeably fewer tabs:

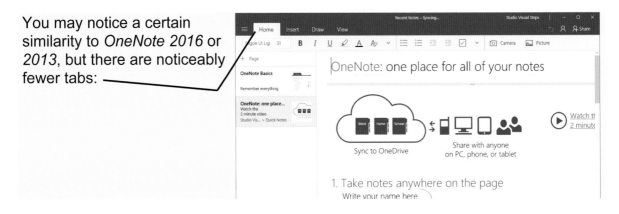

Take a brief look at the differences and some of the new features:

☞ **Click** ▤

The dark left sidebar appears. Here you can search, print and configure your settings. From here you can also open your current notes:

☞ **Click** More Notebooks...

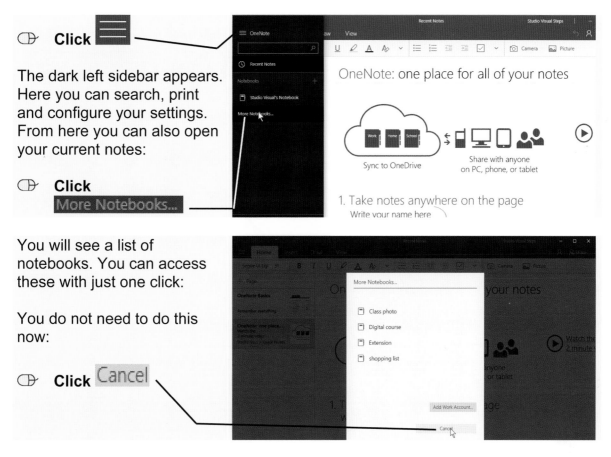

You will see a list of notebooks. You can access these with just one click:

You do not need to do this now:

☞ **Click** Cancel

You can explore the *Insert* tab:

☞ **Click the** | Insert | **tab**

Please note: you can only insert tables, files, images and links.

[O] Camera is a new feature:

The [O] Camera feature lets you make a photograph of a paper document. The document is then straightened, digitized and automatically inserted into *OneNote*. This feature is similar to *Office Lens*, which is discussed further in *section 7.1 Office Lens*.

Now take a look at the *Draw* tab. Here you have the new option of being able to convert drawings into shapes. For example, an oval shape can be transformed into a perfect circle:

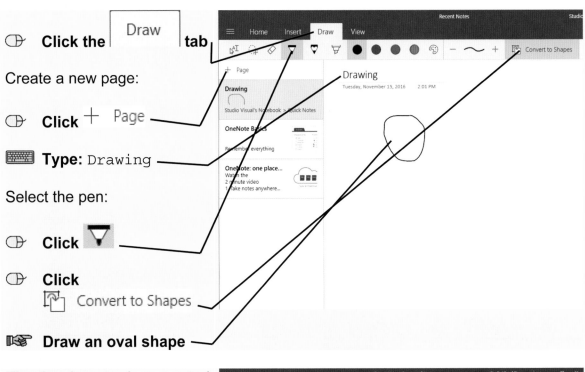

$\oplus$ **Click the** | Draw | **tab**

Create a new page:

$\oplus$ **Click** $+$ Page

⌨ **Type:** Drawing

Select the pen:

$\oplus$ **Click** ▽

$\oplus$ **Click** Convert to Shapes

☞ **Draw an oval shape**

The drawing now is converted into a circle:

This function works for squares and diamonds too:

☞ **Draw a square and a diamond**

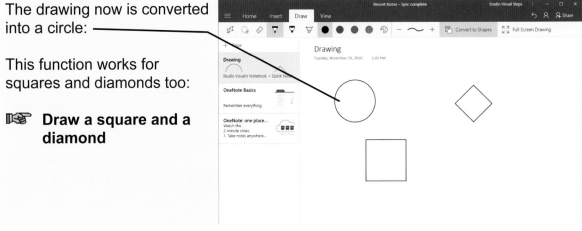

Now take a look at the *View* tab:

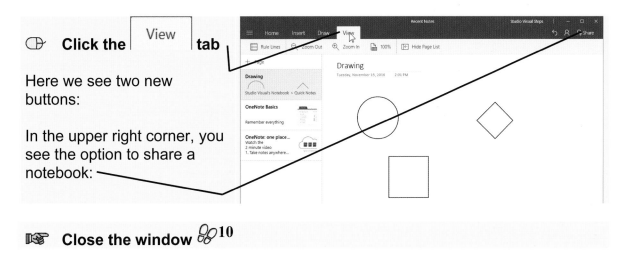

⬚ **Click the** | View | **tab**

Here we see two new buttons:

In the upper right corner, you see the option to share a notebook:

☞ **Close the window** ₰₰10

5.3 Exploring the Web App

The *OneNote* web app is the online version of *OneNote*. It is also called *OneNote Online*. It is available for free and can run in an Internet browser such as *Edge* or *Google Chrome*. The web app is automatically linked to *OneDrive*. When sharing files, you will encounter the web app, so it is a good idea to take a closer look at it now.

You can open the *OneNote* web app as follows:

☞ **Open the web page www.onenote.com/hrd** ₰₰13

The web app requires that you sign in:

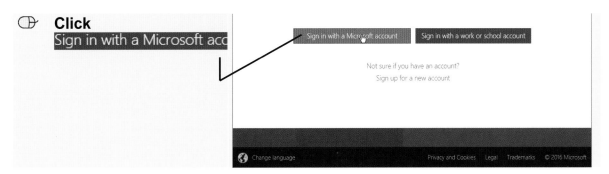

⬚ **Click**
Sign in with a Microsoft acc

Type your email address

Click Next

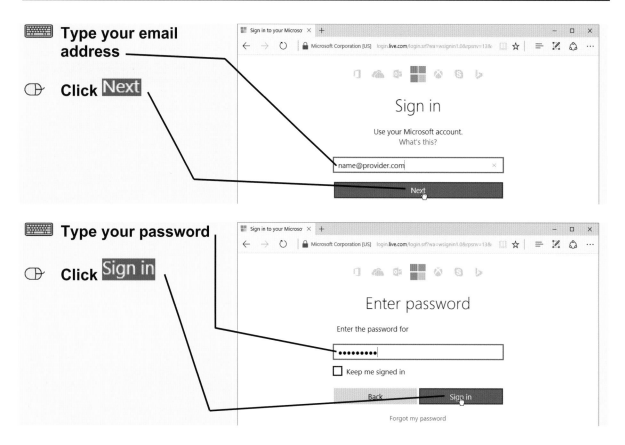

Type your password

Click Sign in

You may see this window:

If necessary, click No thanks

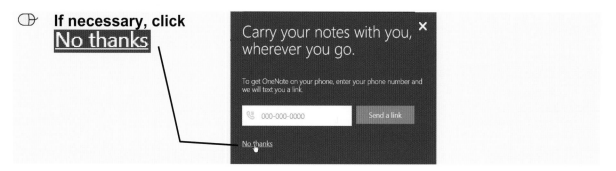

The notebooks stored on *OneDrive* will appear now:

Click shopping list

The notebook is displayed. If you have a small screen, you see that the sections and pages are displayed differently. Furthermore, there is no display of the ribbon with its commands for, for example, text layout or inserting objects. The *OneNote* web app only allows for reading the notebook and not for editing it.

If necessary, you can make the sections and pages visible:

☞ **Click** ≡

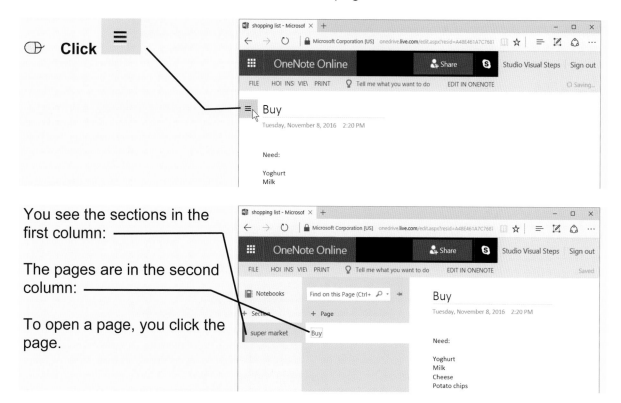

You see the sections in the first column: ─────

The pages are in the second column: ─────

To open a page, you click the page.

There are a few options available:

Printing a notebook: ─────

If a notebook is shared, you can view the users sharing it:

If several people have been working on the notebook, you can see the initials of the authors and the parts they have added and edited by clicking VIEW and 👥.

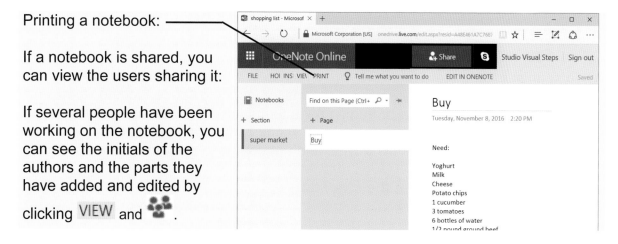

When you receive a link allowing you to edit a notebook or if you are the author of a notebook, you have editing authorization. You can decide whether to perform the editing in a browser or in the *OneNote 2016* or *2013* program. Here is an example of how to edit the notebook:

Click EDIT IN ONENOTE

Select the option for editing in an Internet browser:

Click
Resume editing here

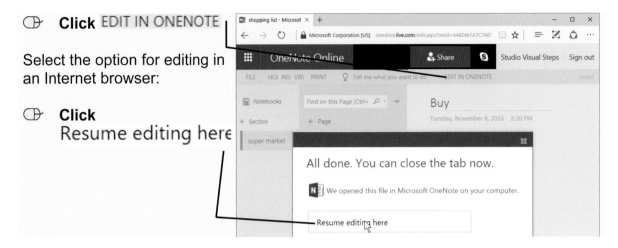

Take a look at some of the editing options for the *OneNote* web app:

To open the ribbon permanently:

Double-click the
HOME **tab**

If anyone else is working on the notebook it will be indicated on the upper right-hand side.

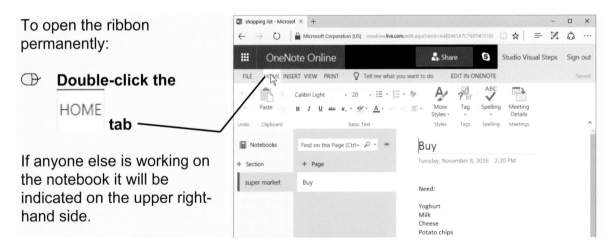

As you can see here, there are fewer options than in the full desktop version of *OneNote 2016* and *2013*. There are no options for inserting space, adding video, changing the color of the page or adding page templates. The web app does not contain a search or drawing option either. Sections cannot be protected and you cannot translate, or search for synonyms and are unable to dock the windows.

☞ **If desired, take a look at the other tabs**

With the edit function you can edit the notebook, but not with the reading only function. You can use the *View* tab to switch between the two views:

Click the VIEW **tab**

Switch between the Editing View and Reading View:

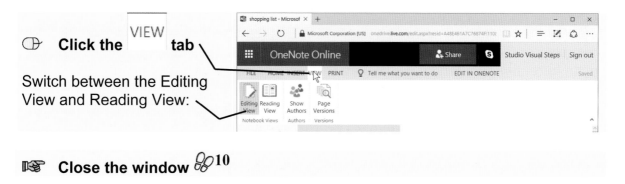

☞ **Close the window** 🐾¹⁰

5.4 OneNote on Mac

OneNote is also available for the Apple user. Since it is unlikely that you are using a Mac, we will only take a brief look at *OneNote for Mac*.

In this example you see the *Movies* notebook opened in *OneNote for Mac*:

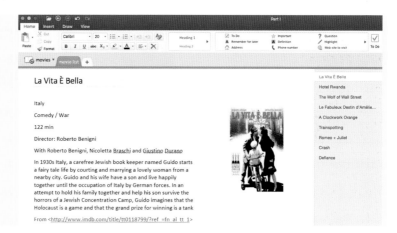

For the most part, *OneNote for Mac* contains the same features as the *OneNote 2016* and *2013* version. However, the options on the *Insert* tab are more limited. For instance, you cannot insert space, add video, rule lines or page templates. Also the *Draw* tab is missing. In addition, you do not have the option for translating or searching for synonyms, and you are unable to dock the windows.

5.5 Sharing a Notebook

The strength of *OneNote* lies in the ability to share notebooks. The person sharing a notebook can make one or two choices: Can Edit (can make changes to the notebook) or Can View (the notebook can only be viewed). Sharing also includes the option to require the person with whom the notebook is shared to sign in.

It is important to realize that a notebook can only be shared if you have saved it on *OneDrive*. If you saved a notebook on your computer, you can still place this on *OneDrive*. Sharing can be done in several ways: by installing a link or by sending an email.

☞ **Open *OneNote*** 🦶¹

☞ **Open the *digital pen* notebook from the *Exercise files OneNote* folder** 🦶11

You now move the notebook from your computer onto *OneDrive*:

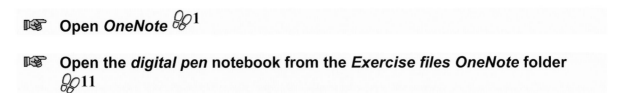

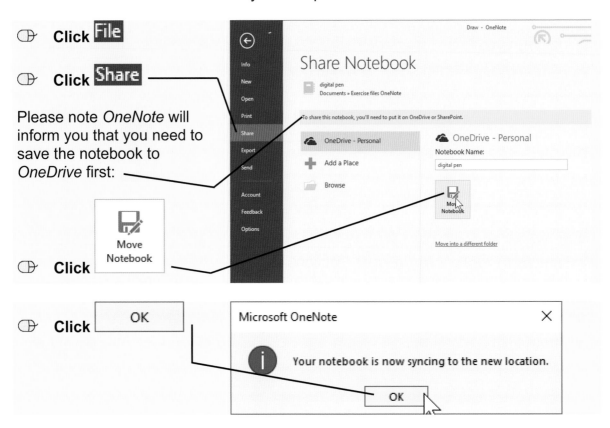

OneNote now places the notebook on *OneDrive* for sharing purposes. You can share the notebook by sending an invitation in an email:

☞ **If necessary, click**

Share with People

Enter the email address of a person you want to share the notebook with:

Tip: if you yourself have multiple email addresses, then fill in one to be able to see the email the receiver will get.

⌨ **Type the desired email address**

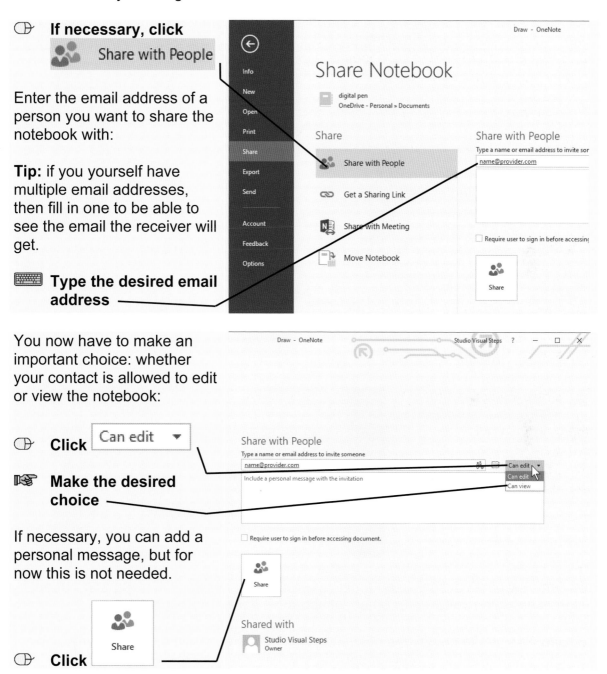

You now have to make an important choice: whether your contact is allowed to edit or view the notebook:

☞ **Click** Can edit ▼

☞ **Make the desired choice**

If necessary, you can add a personal message, but for now this is not needed.

☞ **Click** Share

OneNote will now send an email to the email address. This email contains an invitation to view and possibly edit the notebook.

It is also possible to let *OneNote* generate a link. This will enable others to edit the notebook. This link can be activated on a later date by email as well. Or you can use it to open the notebook on another computer, for a presentation for instance.

☞ **Click**
   ⚭ Get a Sharing Link

You now must determine whether the link will allow the notebook to be edited or just viewed. In this case the option to allow editing is selected:

☞ **By** Edit Link **, click**

   Create an edit link

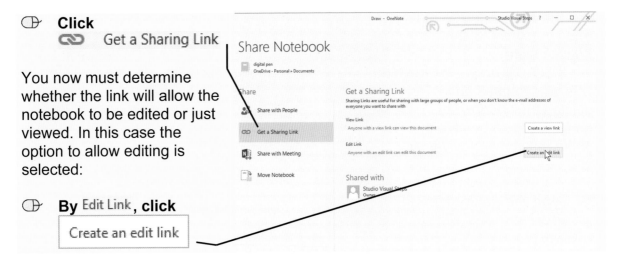

You now see the link. Copy this:

☞ **Right-click the link**
   https://onedrive.live.com/red

☞ **Click** Copy

You can now paste the link in an email program, or share the link using social media, instant messaging software or other collaborative software programs.

You can also create both types of sharing links at the same time, thereby making a distinction between two groups of people, such as teachers and fellow students, by providing editing rights to some and read-only rights to others. If the user opens the link, he or she enters the *OneNote* web app. If you need to, you can review how to edit a notebook in the *OneNote* web app in *section 5.3 Exploring the web app*.

5.6 Synchronizing, Version Control and Trash Can

OneNote tracks all changes. You can go back relatively easy to a prior version of the notebook. This can be important when working with others on the same notebook. If you work together on a single notebook, different versions will appear. From time to time, it will be necessary to make a synchronization, so the changes of the one notebook are displayed in the other notebook as well.

☞ **Open the Internet browser and open the shared notebook by copying the link in the address bar** ❦¹³

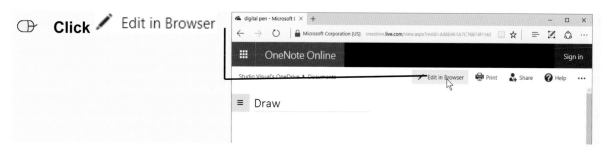

Click ✏ Edit in Browser

For testing the synchronization, you can create a new page in the web app:

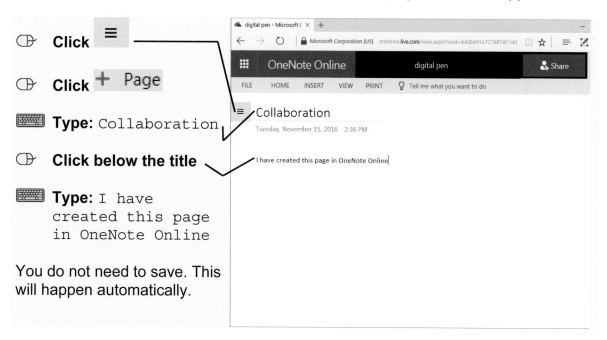

Click ≡

Click + Page

⌨ **Type:** Collaboration

Click below the title

⌨ **Type:** I have
created this page
in OneNote Online

You do not need to save. This will happen automatically.

You will now sync your notebook in *OneNote 2016* or *2013* desktop version. The program should still be open. Normally synchronization happens frequently and automatically.

But sometimes you will want to do this manually:

☞ **If necessary, display the full window in *OneNote*** 🐾**30**

⊕ **If necessary, click**

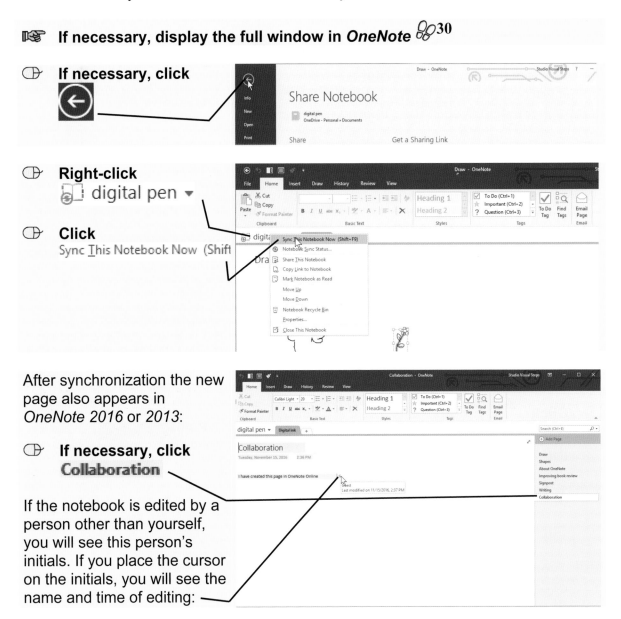

Right-click
🗔 **digital pen** ▼

⊕ **Click**
Sync This Notebook Now (Shift

After synchronization the new page also appears in *OneNote 2016* or *2013*:

⊕ **If necessary, click**
Collaboration

If the notebook is edited by a person other than yourself, you will see this person's initials. If you place the cursor on the initials, you will see the name and time of editing:

Tip

Hiding initials

If the initials of other people distract you, you can hide them:

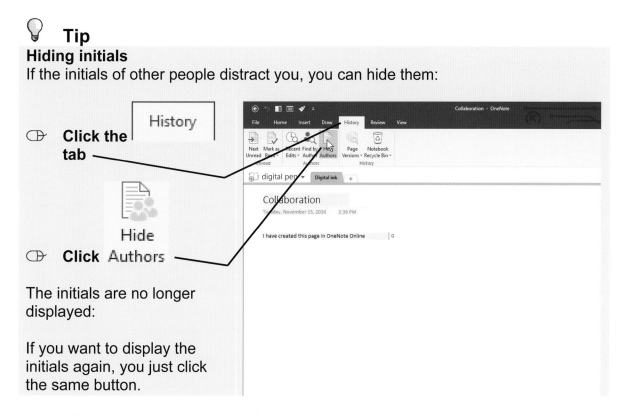

☞ **Click the** History **tab**

☞ **Click** Hide Authors

The initials are no longer displayed:

If you want to display the initials again, you just click the same button.

Several changes have been made to the notebook, you can review them now. In this example it is assumed that the notebook has several authors. That is of course not the case with your own notebook, but you can still follow the next few steps:

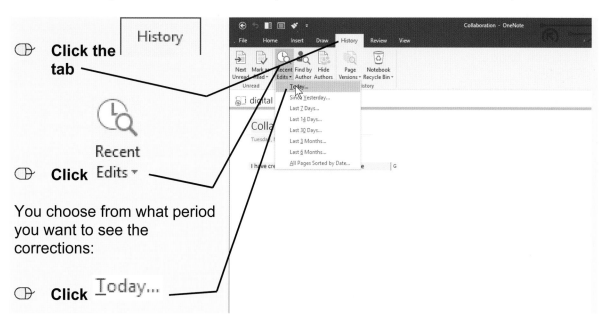

☞ **Click the** History **tab**

☞ **Click** Recent Edits ▾

You choose from what period you want to see the corrections:

☞ **Click** Today...

The corrections from today are highlighted in yellow. You may see other results: ———

On the right-hand side you can search for even more specific changes per page, section or notebook: ———

You now close the *Search Results* pane:

👆 **Click ✕** ————————

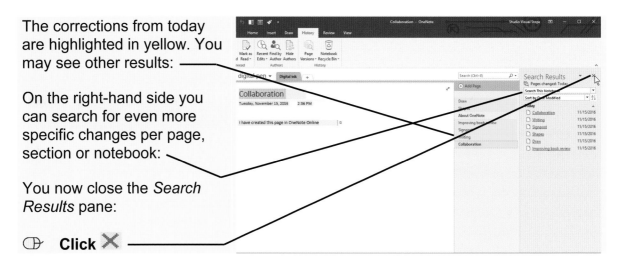

☞ **Close the Internet browser window** 🦶🦶**10**

For the next few procedures you open another notebook:

☞ **Open the *Cookbook* notebook from the *Exercise files OneNote* folder** 🦶🦶**11**

☞ **Make any alteration on the *Pasta with 4 cheeses* page** 🦶🦶**16**, 🦶🦶**9**

Take a look at the page versions:

👆 **Click the** History **tab** ———

👆 **Click** Page Versions ▾ ———

👆 **Click** 🔍 Page Versions ———

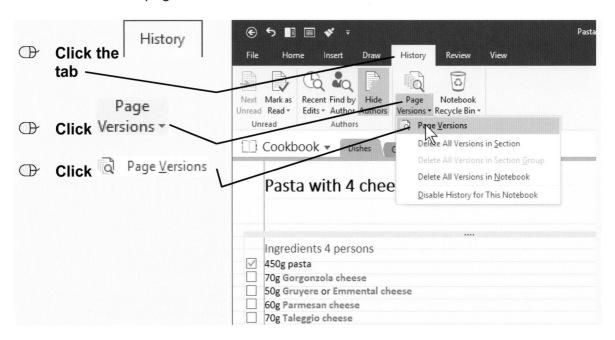

Below the pages you can see its previous versions. This way you can go back to older versions if for instance valuable information is lost. Furthermore, it enables you to see what was added and by whom:

☞ **Click a previous version** ————

You see a previous page version and a notification bar:

If you click this bar, the previous version will be installed and would replace the current page. You do not need to do this now.

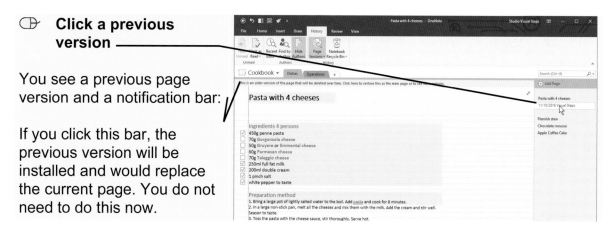

It is also possible to remove the previous versions:

Page
☞ **Click** Versions ▾ ————

You see several options:

If you click Delete All Versions in Section all previous versions in this section will be deleted:

☞ **Click** Delete All Versions in Section

If you click Disable History for This Notebook it will no longer be possible to view a version history for this notebook: ————

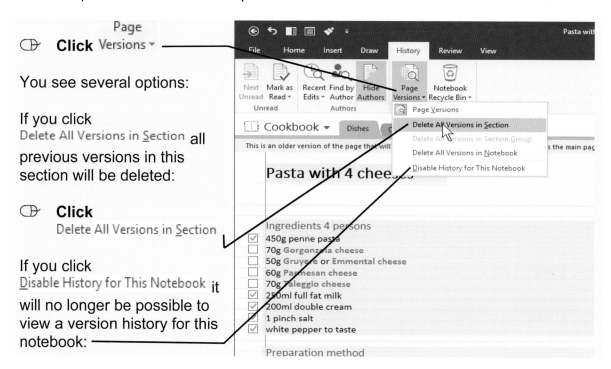

Deleting all the versions in the section has to be confirmed:

☞ **Click** Yes

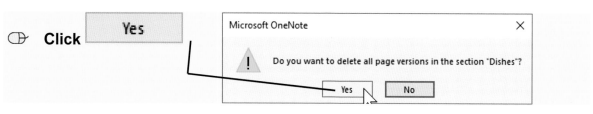

All deleted sections and pages from *OneNote* are first stored in the trash can where they can be retrieved later if needed. You can test this by creating a page, deleting it and then looking for it in the trash can:

☞ **Create a page titled "Test"** 👣6

⌨ **Type:** This is a short test

☞ **Delete the page "Test"** 👣8

🖱 **Click** Notebook Recycle Bin ▾

🖱 **Click** 🗑 Notebook Recycle Bin

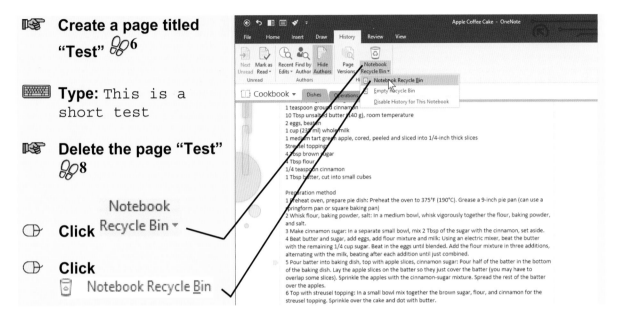

The deleted pages are shown on the right-hand side. You can empty the trash can now:

🖱 **Click** Notebook Recycle Bin ▾

🖱 **Click** 🗑 Empty Recycle Bin

This must be confirmed:

🖱 **Click** Delete

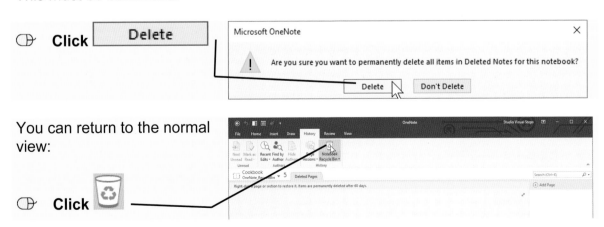

You can return to the normal view:

🖱 **Click** 🗑

Once you have deleted a page permanently you cannot put it back anymore. Also, be aware that items in the trash can are deleted automatically after 60 days.

5.7 A Summary of Your Notebooks

OneNote provides a list where you can sync and share notebooks. You use the *File* tab to do this. Go to the page with a list of your various notebooks:

Click File

Here you see where the notebook is currently saved (on your computer or on *OneDrive*): ————

Viewing the notebook: ————

Sharing the notebook: ————

By a random notebook, click

Settings

Sharing or moving a notebook: ————

Synchronizing a notebook: ————

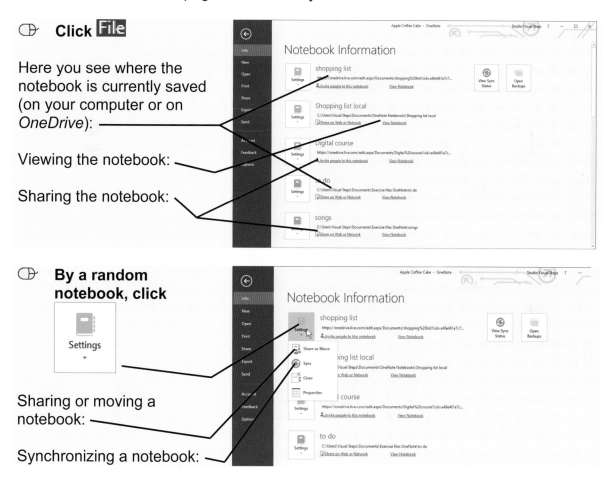

As you can see here, the *Notebook Information* window gives you a short summary of all your notebooks. You can very quickly view, share or synchronize a notebook right from this window.

5.8 Protecting Sections

Even if you share a notebook with others, you may not want everything to be visible. You can protect a section, which can then only be viewed and edited by yourself. This way you can save certain information inside a shared notebook that only you can view:

☞ **Open the *Share* notebook from the *Exercise files OneNote* folder** **11**

➜ **Please note:**
Currently you cannot password protect just a single page. It is also not possible to allow just one user editing or viewing his own section.

In this example, the notebook contains a sketch, photograph and cost calculation to buy a new home. You would like to share the sketch and photo with your friends and family, but prefer to keep the cost calculation to yourself.

You can set a section to be password protected:

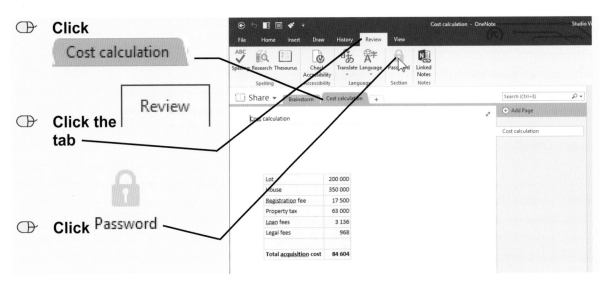

☐	**Click**
	Cost calculation
☐	**Click the tab** *Review*
☐	**Click** *Password*

A new detail pane appears on the right-hand side. Here you create the new password:

☐ **Click** *Set Password...*

Enter the desired password:

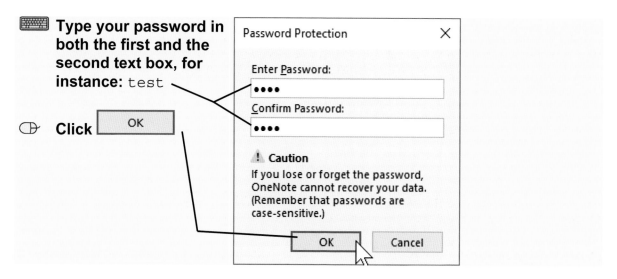

Type your password in both the first and the second text box, for instance: `test`

Click OK

Only when the sections are locked, does the security activate:

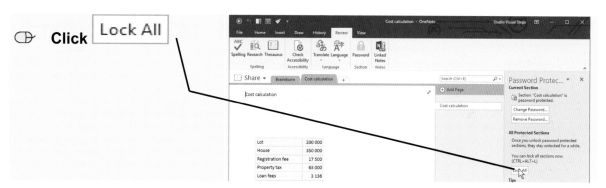

Click Lock All

You now see the notice that the section is protected with a password:

If you want to view or edit this section, click on the left-hand side of the window:

Click the notice

To gain access you need to enter the password:

Type the password in the text box, for instance: `test`

Click OK

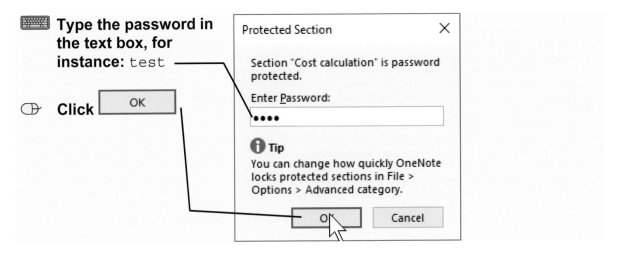

Now you can view the protected section again. You can also remove the password at any time:

If necessary, click

Password

Click

Remove Password...

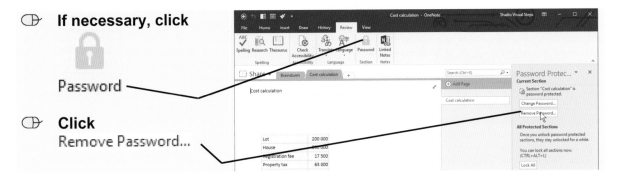

It is only possible to remove a password if you can prove knowing the password:

Type the password in the text box, for instance: `test`

Click OK

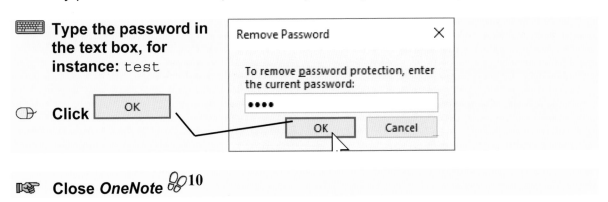

Close *OneNote* ℘10

In this chapter you learned about the different versions of *OneNote*. You have also examined the various methods for sharing a notebook and in addition you have learned how to set up password protection for a particular section of a notebook.

5.9 Exercises

The following exercises will help you master what you have just learned. Have you forgotten how to perform a certain action? The number next to the footsteps tells you where to look it up at the end of the book in the appendix *How Do I Do That Again?*

Exercise 1: Meeting Report

Let's say you are a sport club member and you have regular board meetings. In this exercise you practice making meeting reports in *OneNote*.

☞ Open *OneNote*. 🦶**1**

☞ Create a new notebook, call it *Meeting Report* and save it on *OneDrive*. Do not share the document. 🦶**2**

☞ Name the page: *Members Present*. 🦶**5**

☞ Type the text below the title: `Present: Katie, Vera, Michel, James` 🦶**9**

☞ You decide after all to work with a page template. You can delete the *Members Present* page. 🦶**8**

☞ Make a new page from the page template *Simple Meeting Notes 2* (located in the Business category). 🦶**24**

☞ You forgot who was present at the meeting and need to look for these members in the trash can. 🦶**50**

☞ Empty the trash can. 🦶**51**

☞ Add the following text to the page. 🐾⁹

> ### Meeting Sport club
> Tuesday, November 15, 2016　　　4:23 PM
>
> ⋯⋯
>
> **Agenda:**
> 1. Recruiting new members
> 2. Club party
> 3. Discuss budget
>
> **Attendees:**
> ○ Katie
> ○ Vera
> ○ Michel
> ○ James
>
> **Action Items:**
> ☐ We have to recruit new members. We start with an advertisement on Facebook and in the paper.

☞ Create an editable link and copy this link. 🐾⁵²

☞ Open the report in the Internet browser by clicking the copied link in *OneNote Online*. 🐾¹³

☞ Edit the report in the Internet browser. 🐾⁵³

☞ Add a new page and name this *Reflections*. 🐾⁵⁴

☞ Below the title, type the text: `The budget seems to be incomplete and unachievable.` 🐾⁹

☞ Close the Internet browser. 🐾¹⁰

☞ Return to *OneNote*. 🐾³⁰

☞ Sync the notebook so the new page is visible here as well. 🐾⁵⁵

☞ Close *OneNote*. 🐾¹⁰

5.10 Background Information

Glossary

App	App is short for *application*. This means a program or application. An app was originally a program for a tablet or smartphone. But in *Windows*, you can also use apps on your computer.
Synchronizing	Literally: blending or equalizing. Turning information from different *OneNote* versions into the same information in every version by copying the information to and fro.
Web app	A web app is an application or program that works in an Internet browser.

Source: help function of OneNote, Wikipedia

Special shared document

As you have seen, *OneNote* is an ideal program for sharing notebooks. The following notebook has been shared around the world, and dozens of teachers signed in their own language a simple greeting "Hello". A nice detail is that Chris Pratley, the person who made *OneNote*, signed the document too:

5.11 Tips

 Tip

Apps for iOS and Android

There are apps available for *iOS* and *Android*. This means you can also make use of *OneNote* on your iPad, iPhone, *Android* tablet or *Android* smartphone. *OneNote* is also available on the *Windows* Phone. After logging in, your notebooks are automatically synchronized with your *OneDrive* account.

You can download the apps from the *App Store* on your iPad or iPhone or in the *Play Store* on your *Android* tablet or *Android* smartphone:

Here you see *OneNote* on the iPad:

The sections and pages are displayed here:

You can see that the app, in comparison to the program on a computer, has fewer options:

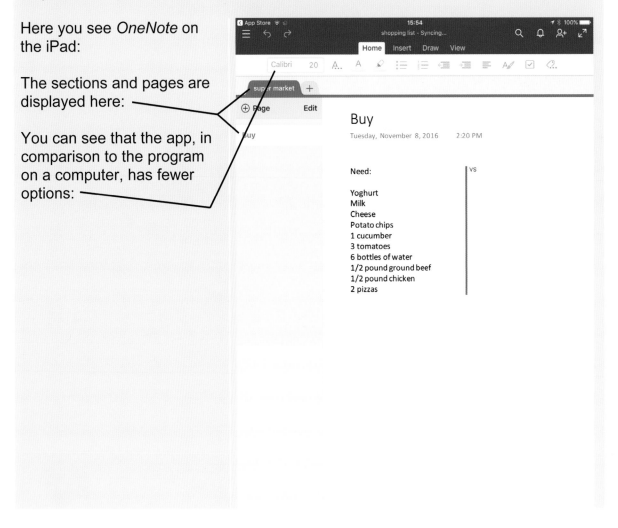

6. Exporting, Printing, Translating and More

In this chapter you will learn how to export or print a page, section or complete notebook. You will also learn how to send pages by email. In addition, you will translate text, look up the meaning of difficult words and search for synonyms.

In this chapter you learn how to:

- export;
- print;
- send pages by email;
- translate text;
- look up the meaning of difficult words;
- search for synonyms.

6.1 Exporting

OneNote does not use the *Word* file type extension .DOC or .DOCX and that may take some getting used to. *OneNote* saves each notebook in a separate folder in the *Documents > OneNote Notebooks* folder. This folder contains several files per section. It is possible to export your notebooks to .DOCX, .DOC, .PDF or .ONE files. You have the choice of exporting an entire notebook, a section or a single page.

☞ **Open *OneNote*** **1**

☞ **Open the *Research* notebook from the *Exercise files OneNote* folder** **11**

You see the *OneNote* notebook named *Research*:

👆 **Click File**

In this example, choose the option to export a file from the current section to a PDF file. Note that you are only given the choice to export a page or the entire notebook. You can choose among several file types.

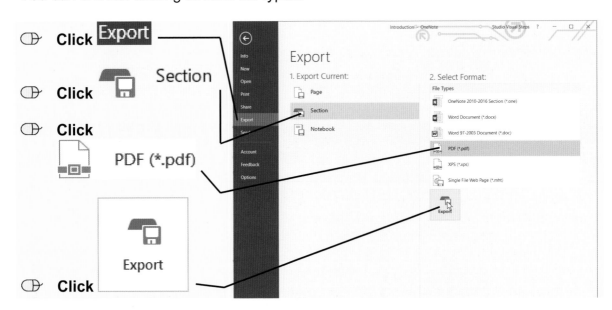

👆 **Click Export**

👆 **Click** **Section**

👆 **Click**
PDF (*.pdf)

👆 **Click** **Export**

If you want to export to a *Word*-document, choose **Word Document (*.docx)** or
 Word 97-2003 Document (*.doc)

You can save the PDF in the *Documents* folder:

☞ **Click** 📑 **Documents**

☞ **Click** | Save |

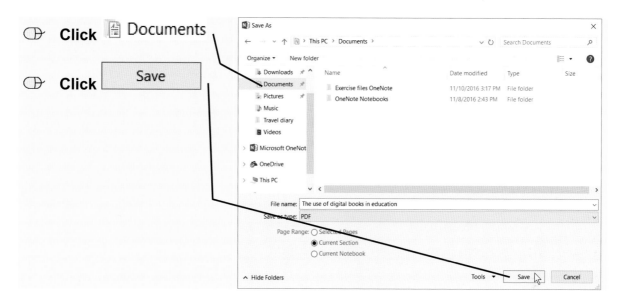

Now you can open the PDF file:

☞ **Open** *File Explorer* ✋⁵⁶

☞ **Click** 📑 **Documents**

☞ **Double-click**
  📄 **The use of digital books in**

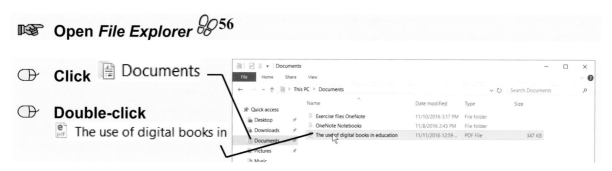

In this example the file is opened in the Internet browser *Edge*. Your computer may have a different setting that opens PDF files in a program such as *Adobe Acrobat Reader*.

Nothing is lost when converting to PDF. Both text, digital ink and images are saved in the PDF file:

You can close the PDF file:

☞ **Click** ✕

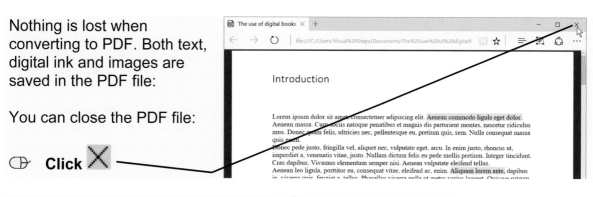

☞ **If necessary, close** *File Explorer* ✋¹⁰

You now see the *OneNote* window again.

 Tip
Exporting a notebook from OneDrive to your computer
If you have a notebook stored on *OneDrive* and really want to save it to your computer, then you can export the notebook. Please note that if you make adjustments to the notebook on your computer, it will not update automatically on *OneDrive*. In this example an entire notebook is exported. This is also possible for a single page or section.

Next, you can select the folder for the exported file. This could be, for example, the *Documents > OneNote Notebooks* folder.

6.2 Printing

In *OneNote* you can take a look at the print preview to see how the information will be printed on paper:

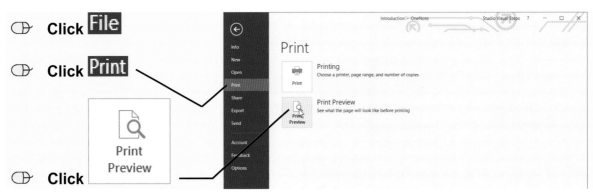

You can choose whether to print the page or the section:

Choose the paper size:

Change the print orientation:

You can also choose whether you see a footer and select its style:

To print the file:

⊕ **Click** Print...

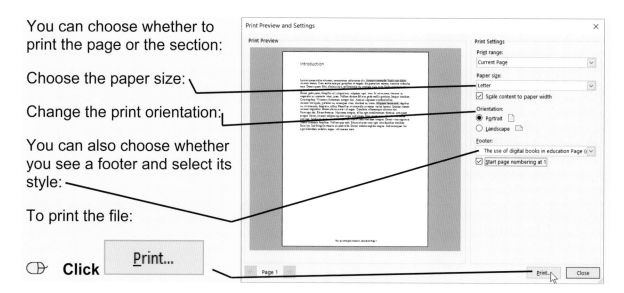

The *Print* window appears:

⊕ **Click the desired printer**

If necessary, you can specify which pages you would like to print. These are the page numbers you see at the bottom of the print preview:

Enter the number of copies:

You can print the file:

⊕ **Click** Print...

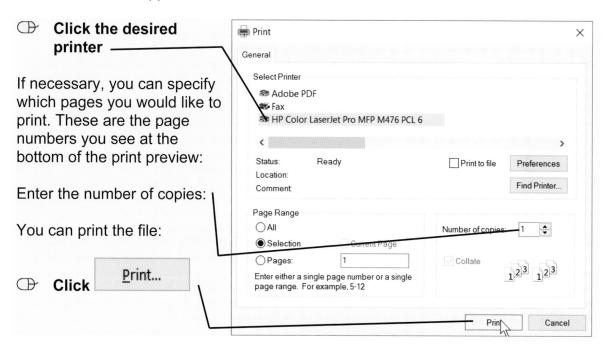

The notebook is printed.

6.3 Translating

If you work on a notebook with people of various nationalities, you may be confronted with foreign languages. *OneNote* includes a translation feature:

☞ **Open the page named *Approch*** 🦶🦶**16**

You can translate a word from English to Portuguese:

☞ **Select the word "yellow"** 🦶🦶**12**

⊕ **Click the** Review **tab**

⊕ **Click** Translate ▾

⊕ **Click**
   Translate Selected Text
   Translate the selected text i
   different language

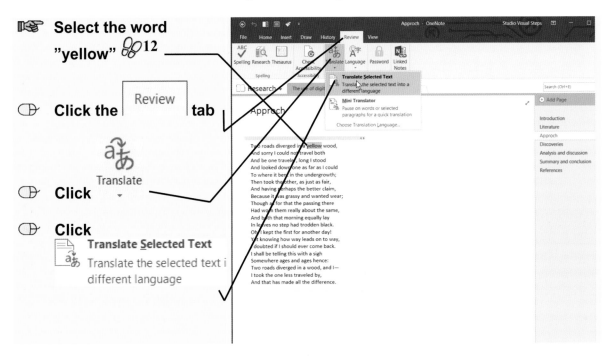

The translation is provided by the *Microsoft* Translator software. For translation purposes, the text is sent in a secure format to *Microsoft*. You need to confirm this:

⊕ **Click** Yes

Then you need to install the appropriate languages:

🖱 **By** From**, select**
English (United States)

🖱 **By** To**, select**
Portuguese (Brazil)

The translation now appears:

To replace the word:

🖱 **Click** | Insert |

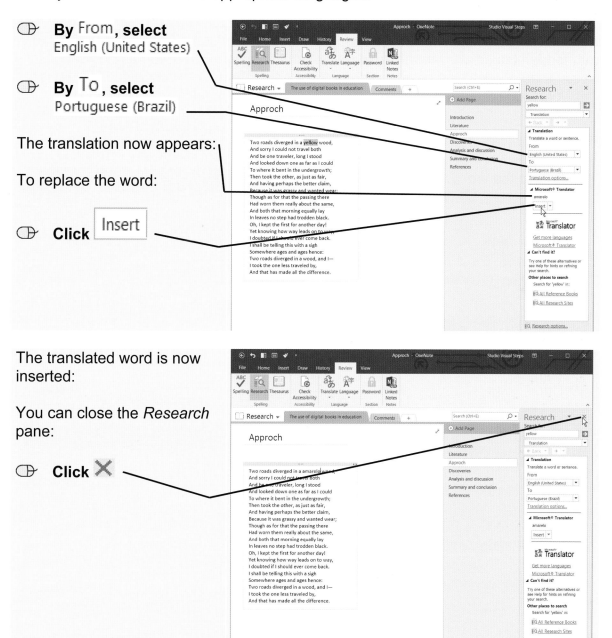

The translated word is now inserted:

You can close the *Research* pane:

🖱 **Click** ✕

You can also translate whole sentences. Just be aware that at the time of writing this book, the translation software that is available is not yet perfect. If you need to work more often in a language other than English, you may want to consider clicking the *Language* button in the *Review* group and setting the proofing language to the one you need.

6.4 Research

When reading complex or difficult text, you may run across an unfamiliar word. This can happen especially with an academic or scholarly work but even a newspaper article, a poetry work or a digital resource may contain words you do not understand. *OneNote* has a feature that allows you to look up the explanation of difficult words.

☞ **Open the page named *Analysis and discussion*** 🦶🦶16

☞ **Select the word** knowledge 🦶🦶12

⊖ **Click** Research

⊖ **By** Translation, **click** ▼

⊖ **Click** Bing

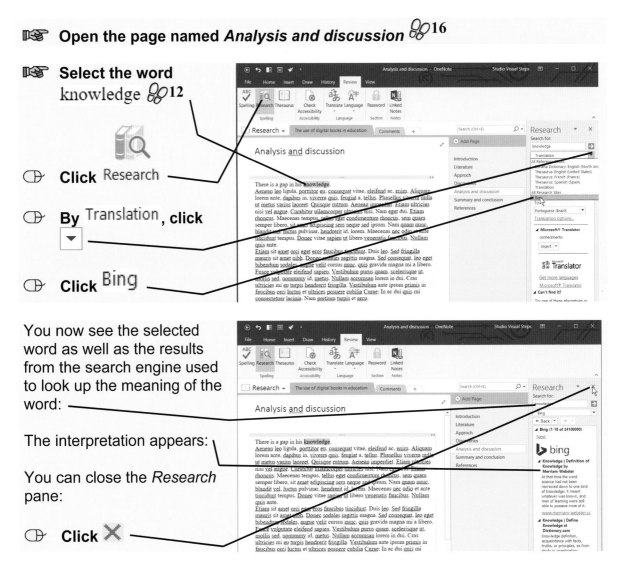

You now see the selected word as well as the results from the search engine used to look up the meaning of the word:

The interpretation appears:

You can close the *Research* pane:

⊖ **Click** ✕

The *Bing* search engine searches for various interpretations on websites such as encyclo.com, wikipedia.org and vocabulary.com.

6.5 Synonyms

When writing a text, you may notice that you use the same word over and over again. A well-constructed text will often contain synonyms, variations of particular words. *OneNote* can generate these synonyms and give you some inspiration:

☞ **Open the page named *Summary and conclusion*** 🦶🦶16

In the first section the same word appears twice. You can search for a synonym:

☞ **Select the word study** 🦶🦶12

Click Thesaurus

By default, English (United States) is selected:

You see a list with various synonyms:

You can close the *Thesaurus* pane:

👉 **Click** ✖

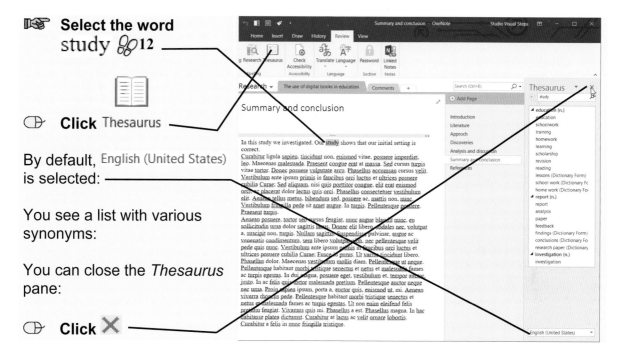

6.6 Sending a Page by Email

Another great feature in *OneNote* is the ability to send pages by email. To use this feature, there needs to be an email account set up in the *Microsoft Outlook* email program.

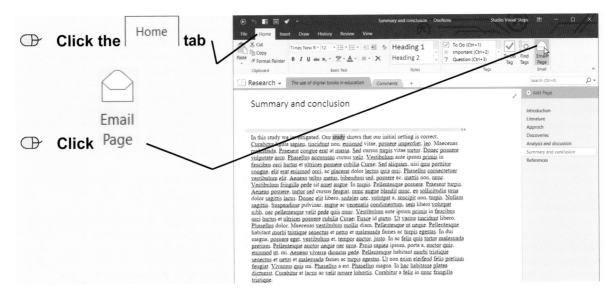

☞ **Click the** Home **tab**

Click Email Page

A new message window appears in *Outlook*. The content of the *OneNote* page already fills the text box. Close the window:

☞ **Click** ✖

☞ **Close** *OneNote* ✂ 10

In this chapter you have learned how to export pages, sections and notebooks to PDF. For *Word* documents, this can be done pretty much in the same way. You have also seen the possibilities for printing and sending pages by email. In addition, you have taken a look at a number of options for more advanced text processing in *OneNote*, such as translation and word lookup to find a definition or synonym.

6.7 Exercises

The following exercises will help you master what you have just learned. Have you forgotten how to perform a certain action? The number next to the footsteps tells you where to look it up at the end of the book in the appendix *How Do I Do That Again?*

Exercise 1: Procedures

You open a notebook that contains a poem in multiple languages and some difficult words. You can translate the sentences and search for words and synonyms. Then you can export the poem and print it.

☞ Open *OneNote.* ぺ**1**

☞ Open the *Procedures* notebook from the *Exercise files OneNote* folder. ぺ**11**

☞ Translate the sentence "To look back on" (ninth line) from English to Dutch. ぺ**57**

☞ Search for a synonym for "music" (sixteenth line). ぺ**58**

☞ Research the word "intersections" (fourth line). ぺ**59**

☞ Export the section "Short stories" to a PDF file. ぺ**60**

☞ Take a look at the print preview and print the poem "The afterlife of fame". ぺ**61**

☞ Close *OneNote.* ぺ**10**

6.8 Background Information

Glossary

Bing	*Microsoft* search engine. *Bing* also contains a translation service.
Exporting	Saving data in another file type.
PDF file	PDF stands for Portable Document Format. This is a file format for digital documents.
Print preview	Option that allows users to view how a printed notebook will look on paper on their computer screen.
Synonym	A word with a similar meaning.

Source: OneNote help function, Wikipedia

7. Extending OneNote

There are many interesting extensions for *OneNote*. Extensions, also known as plug-ins or add-ins, give additional functionality to *OneNote*.

This chapter discusses some of the interesting features of the *OneTastic* plug-in. It not only lets you crop photos, you can also use it to create, run and download macros. By using macros you can automate certain processes in your notebooks.

We also discuss the *Office Lens* app. This app can be installed on your smartphone or tablet. It can be used to scan documents and it will automatically straighten them. They can then be imported into *OneNote*.

The *Gem* plug-in is a sort of toolkit that gives lots of extra features to *OneNote*. *Gem* offers at least five additional tabs. You can try a thirty day free trial, after that it is a paid service.

OneNote Publisher for WordPress lets you quickly import *OneNote* pages into a *WordPress* website. And thanks to the *Sway Add-In for OneNote*, you can quickly convert a *OneNote* page into a *Sway* presentation. *Sway* is a free service that lets you create and share online presentations. *Email to OneNote* lets you quickly add the content from an email to a *OneNote* notebook.

In this chapter you learn how to:

- digitize documents with *Office Lens*;
- download and use extra options with *OneTastic*;
- add extra options with the *Gem* plug-in;
- add extra options with the *OneNote Publisher for WordPress* plug-in;
- convert a page to *Sway* with the *Sway Add-in for OneNote*;
- add pages to *OneNote* by email.

7.1 Office Lens

Office Lens is not an extension in *OneNote* itself but it is related to *OneNote*. The app is available for the iPhone, *Android* phones and the *Windows Phone*. For example, you can use it to take a picture of a document, photo, whiteboard or business card. The shape of this photo will then automatically be corrected and straightened. It can then be sent in an email, saved as a photo or PDF file, or exported to *OneNote*, *Word* and *PowerPoint*. *Office Lens* makes a great alternative when a scanner is not available.

Office Lens can be downloaded for free from http://aka.ms/officelens. The web page will guide you to the right location where you can subsequently install the app.

☞ **Download the *Office Lens* app onto your smartphone**

In *Chapter 5 Sharing notebooks* you learned a little about the *OneNote* app in *Windows 10*. *Office Lens* is a built-in feature in *Windows 10*.

☞ **Open *OneNote* 👣[1]**

☞ **Create a new notebook on *OneDrive* called *Extension*, but do not share this notebook 👣[2]**

With *Office Lens* you now can scan and export a document to *OneNote*. You can choose the type of scan you want to perform: a scan of a document, photo, whiteboard or business card.

➥ **Please note:**

The following screen shots were made with an iPhone. It works in a similar way on an *Android* phone or *Windows* Phone.

☞ **Open the *Office Lens* app on your smartphone**

The document will be recognized automatically. *Office Lens* sets a white frame around the document:

To make the photograph:

☞ **Tap**

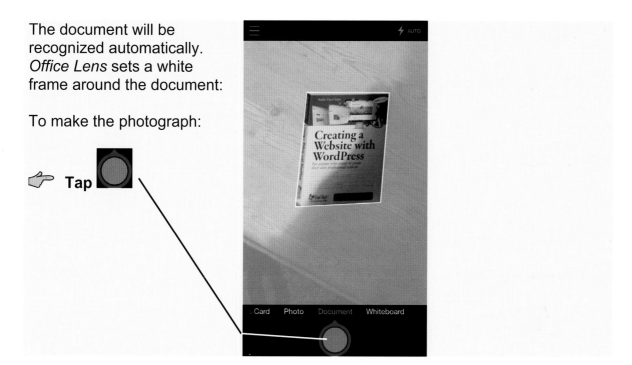

The document will be straightened automatically:

If you are not satisfied with your picture, you can delete it and try again with :

In one session you can create up to ten photographs. These are all put on one page.

If *Office Lens* does not recognize the document, you can add the frame yourself with :

If you are satisfied:

☞ **Tap** Done

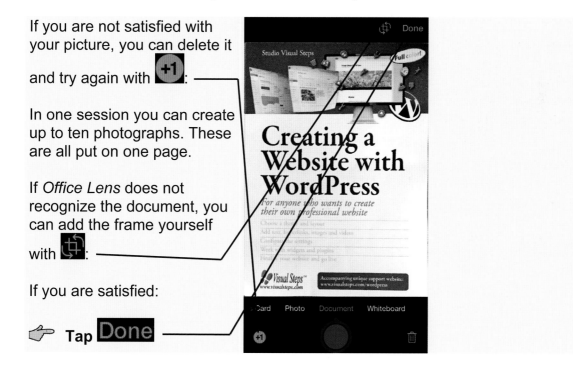

You can choose what you want to do with the scan. For example, export it to *OneNote*, save it as a PDF file, send it as an email or save it as a picture:

In this example, we use the export to *OneNote* option.

👉 **Tap** OneNote

👉 **Type your email address**

👉 **Tap** Next

👉 **Type your password**

👉 **Tap** Sign in

👉 **By** Title**, type a page title**

The location of the last opened notebook is shown here by default. If this is not the right location, you can select a different one:

👉 **Tap** Location

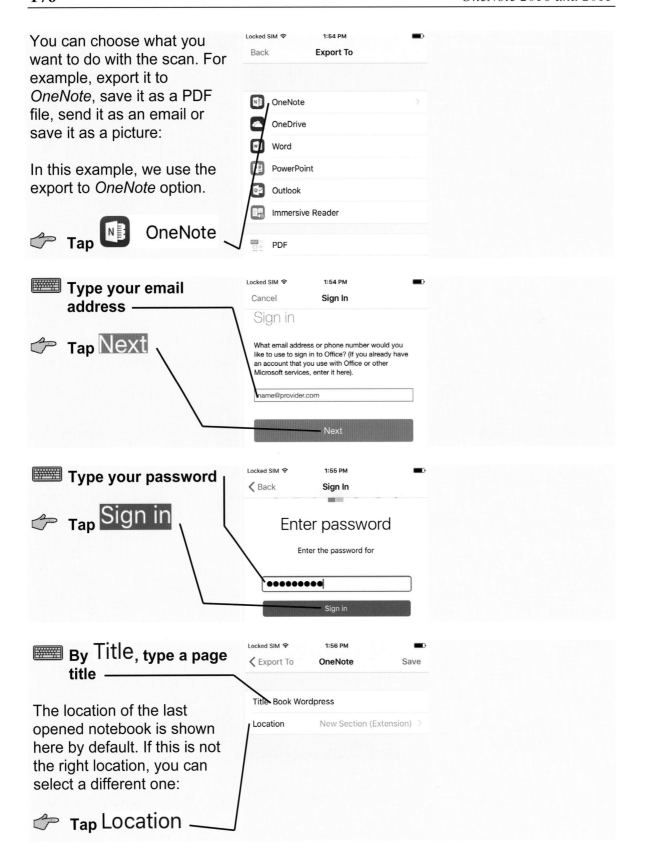

Now you can set up the notebook and section where the scan will be exported to:

☞ **Tap** Extension

☞ **Tap the desired section**

Here you see your chosen location:

Now you can save the scan:

☞ **Tap Save**

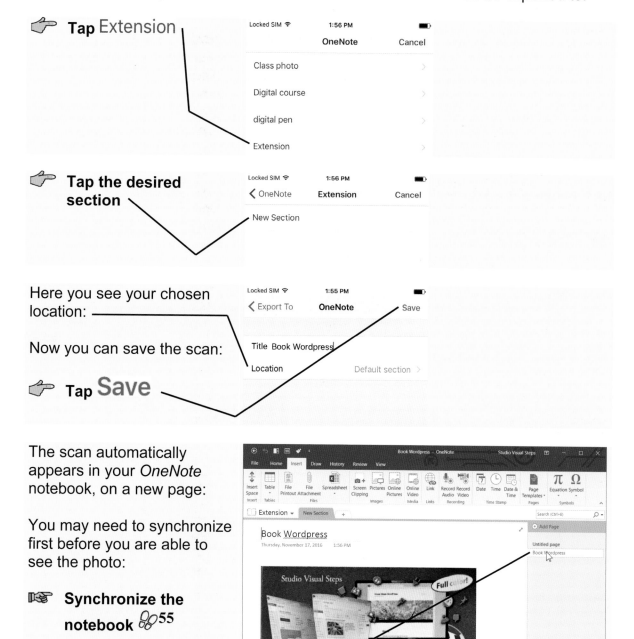

The scan automatically appears in your *OneNote* notebook, on a new page:

You may need to synchronize first before you are able to see the photo:

☞ **Synchronize the notebook** ✍️⁵⁵

☞ **If necessary, click the page**

You have now learned how easy it is to scan and export a photo to *OneNote* with the *Office Lens* app.

7.2 OneTastic

OneTastic is a plug-in (or add-in) application that can be installed into *OneNote.* It gives *OneNote* lots of new features. With *OneTastic* you can crop images, do more with image styles, search and replace words, create calendars and create links from your desktop. You can also use it to create, run and download macros.

In the next few steps we cover the procedure for installing the *OneTastic* plug-in. *OneNote* needs to be closed for this:

☞ **Close *OneNote* 🦶🦶10**

☞ **Open the website www.omeratay.com/onetastic 🦶🦶13**

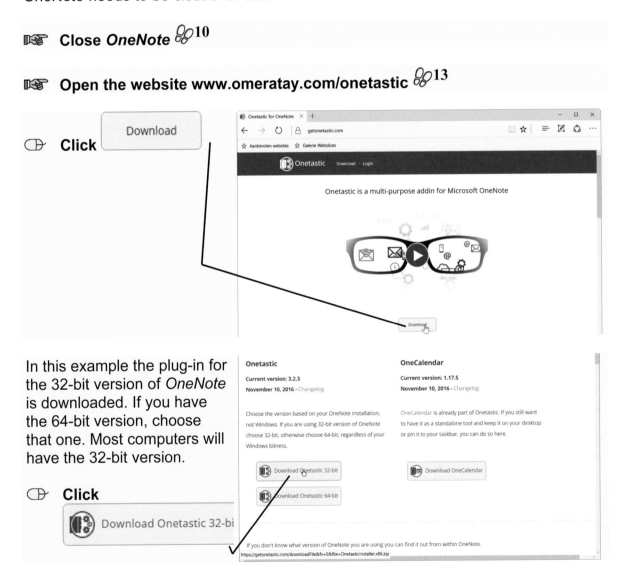

In this example the plug-in for the 32-bit version of *OneNote* is downloaded. If you have the 64-bit version, choose that one. Most computers will have the 32-bit version.

👉 **Check the box** ☑ **by**
   I agree with the license terms

👉 **Click** Download

You will be asked to save the file:

👉 **Click** Save

The file is downloaded. Now you can open the file:

👉 **Click** Open

You can see the *Downloads* folder with the actual downloaded file:

👉 **Double-click**
   🔲 OnetasticInstaller

You see the window below:

If the correct language is
selected: ——————

👉 **Click**
   Continue >

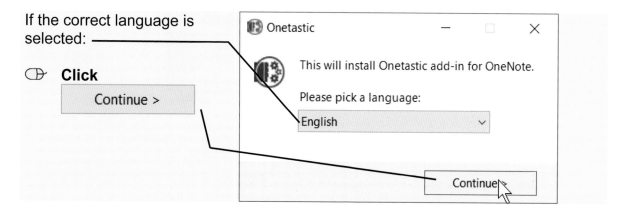

Once the installation is complete, you can open *OneNote*:

⊕ **Click**

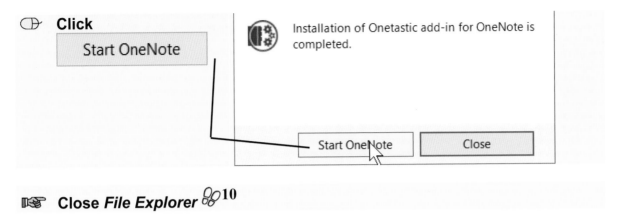

☞ **Close** *File Explorer* ⚜️**10**

Now that *OneTastic* is installed, you can explore some of its new options. Take a look at the new buttons on the tabs:

⊕ **If necessary, click the**

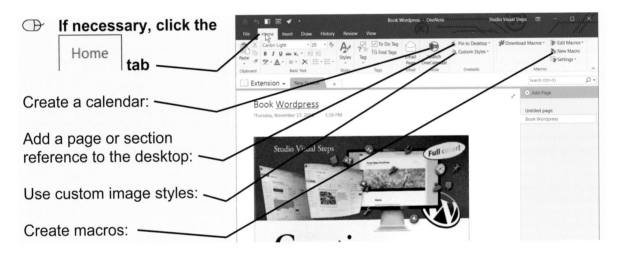

Home **tab**

Create a calendar:

Add a page or section
reference to the desktop:

Use custom image styles:

Create macros:

Here you can see an example of the option to crop images:

⊕ **Right-click the image**

⊕ **Click** ⊞ Crop

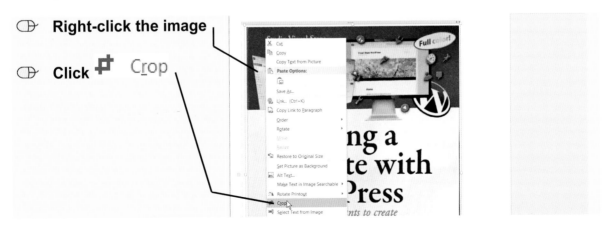

You will see a new window in which the image can be cropped:

By dragging the handles
along the corners and edges,
you can select the area of the
image to be cropped:

☞ **Drag the handles
towards the center
below the image**

If you are satisfied:

☞ **Click** Accept

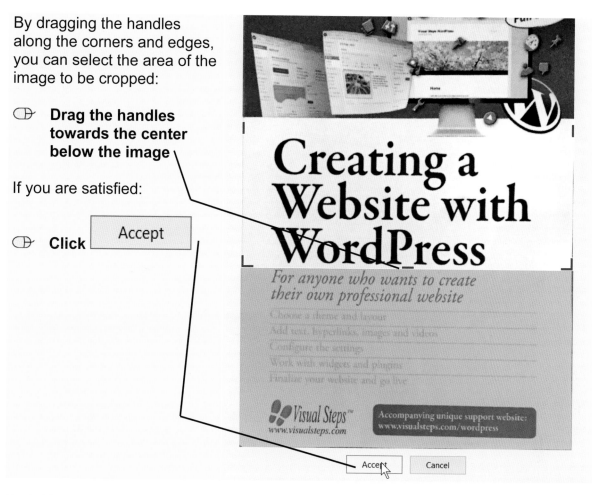

The image has been cropped:

☞ **Open the *Research* notebook from the *Exercise files OneNote* folder** ✂11

You can use macros in *OneNote* to automate many tasks. Macros can be almost as broad and strong as programs themselves. Since macros are this extensive, you have to open them as a separate tab.

☞ **Open the page**
   Introduction 🦶16

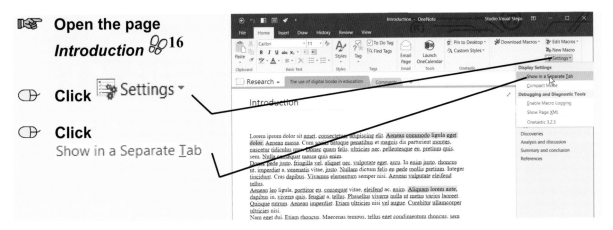

☞ **Click** 🖭 Settings ▾

☞ **Click**
   Show in a Separate Tab

You now see the new *Macros* tab. Here is a short overview of available options:

☞ **If necessary, click the**
   Macros **tab**

Download macros:

Edit macro:

Create macro:

Settings for the tab:

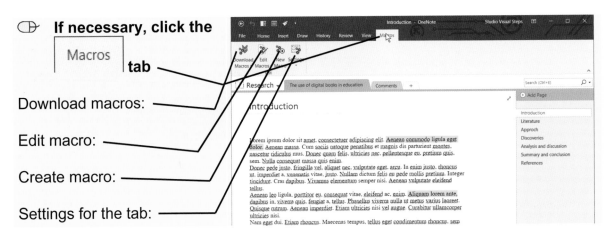

New

With the Macro button you would be able to create new macros yourself. This can be quite complicated and it is not advisable to do this until you have gained some experience. Luckily, on the *OneTastic* website there are many free and ready-to-use macros available.

☞ **Open the web page http://www.omeratay.com/onetastic/?r=macroland**
   🦶13

In this example, we show you how to download the *TOC in Current Notebook* macro. This feature gives you the option to create a table of contents:

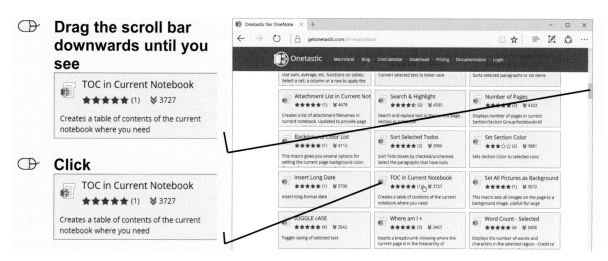

You will be sent to the page for this specific macro:

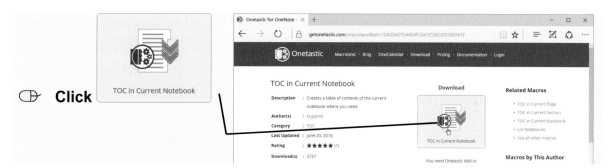

You will need to agree to the license terms:

You first need to save the macro file, then you can open it:

Click Open

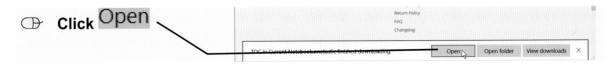

You will be asked to continue:

Click Yes

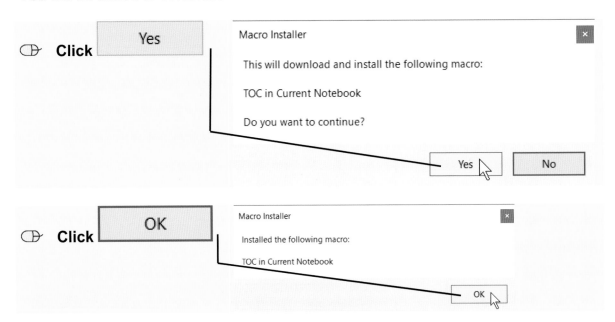

Click OK

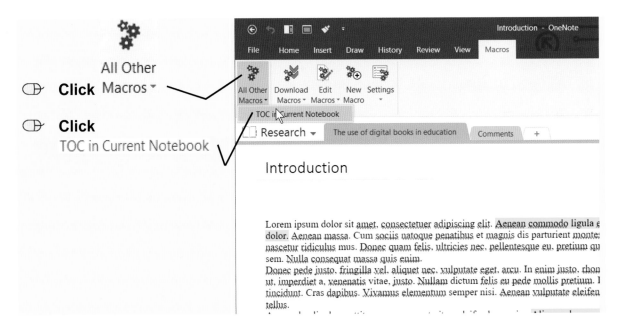

You now see the new macro in *OneNote*. You can run the macro:

Click All Other Macros ▾

Click TOC in Current Notebook

The macro creates a new page with a table of contents:

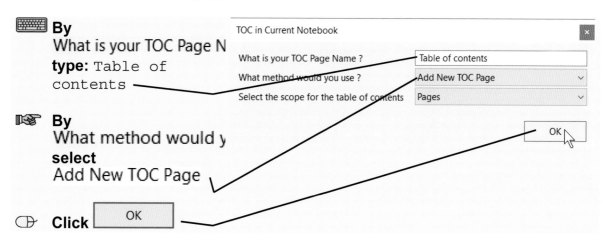

⌨ **By**
What is your TOC Page N
type: `Table of`
`contents`

☞ **By**
What method would y
select
Add New TOC Page

🖰 **Click** OK

The table of contents is inserted into a new page:

The links are clickable and refer to the different pages within the document:

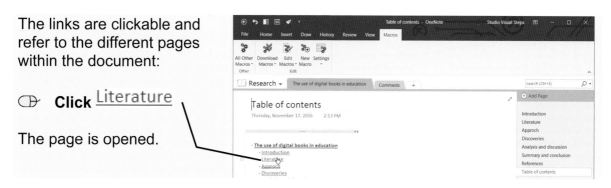

🖰 **Click** Literature

The page is opened.

Plug-ins can also be deactivated. You can deactivate a plug-in via *Options* in *OneNote*:

🖰 **Click** File

🖰 **Click** Options

You will see the plug-in (add-ins) summary page. Here you can see which applications are active and which are inactive:

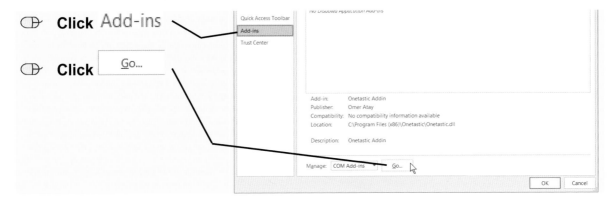

You can turn off the *OneTastic Addin*:

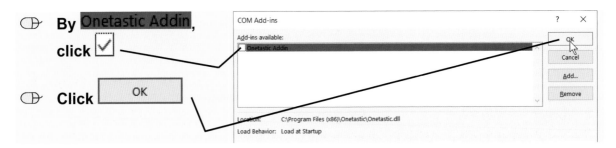

The plug-in is no longer active.

☞ **Close *OneNote*** ᨎ[10]

In this section you have learned how to install and activate the *OneTastic* plug-in. It enabled you to crop images and run macros. You have also seen how to download and install a ready-made macro.

7.3 Other plug-ins

Gem is an extensive plug-in or toolkit that gives *OneNote* many extra features. They include making a quick back up, counting signs and words, folding pages, inserting horizontal lines, making a calendar, quickly enlarging and minimizing text, installing backgrounds, converting photos into black and white, doing more with links, inserting icons, exporting tables to *Excel*, inserting slideshows, setting up auto correct, inserting mathematical formulas, inserting a table of contents, making to do lists, sorting sections and pages alphabetically, sorting tables, showing alerts when files are too large, and much more.

You can download a free trial version for 30 days from http://www.onenotegem.com

Gem offers at least five new tabs:

Gem will not be further discussed here.

OneNote Publisher for WordPress is a free plug-in that can be installed in a website created with *WordPress*. *WordPress* is a popular, free Content Management System for building websites.

You can use this plug-in to import a page from *OneNote* into your website with just a few mouse clicks. This can save you a lot of time. Both text and images are copied to the web page. *OneNote Publisher for WordPress* can be downloaded from https://wordpress.org/plugins/onenote-publisher

Once installed to *WordPress* you will see a new button for adding a page from *OneNote* :

Next, you can choose the desired page to import in the following window.

This plug-in will not be further discussed here.

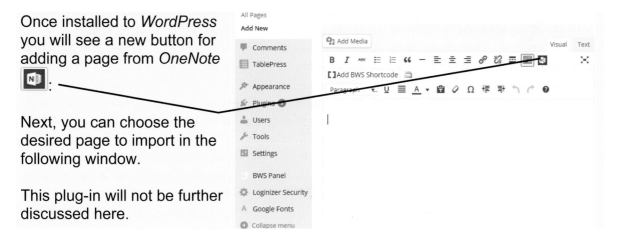

Sway is a free service for building online presentations, called *Sways*. *Sway* is user friendly and rather helpful in making a layout and reordering the content. As the presentations are saved online, they can easily be shared and edited by several authors at the same time. You can use *Sway* via www.sway.com. Once you have logged in with your *Microsoft* account you can start making presentations right away.

Sway has invented a new way of adding content. In most programs, you layout the text and images with a WYSIWYG editor. WYSIWYG means What You See Is What You Get. *Sway* however, uses the WYGIWYW principle: What You Get Is What You Want. *Sway* will take care of the needed layout and makes sure that the presentation is correctly shown on a computer or tablet as well as a smartphone. Nice to know: *Sway* was developed by the same person that created *OneNote*: Chris Pratley.

With the *Sway Add-In for OneNote* you can quickly convert a *OneNote* page to *Sway*. The *Sway Add-In for OneNote* can be downloaded from https://www.microsoft.com/en-us/download/details.aspx?id=50418

☞ **Open the web page https://www.microsoft.com/en-us/download/details.aspx?id=50418** ✂¹³

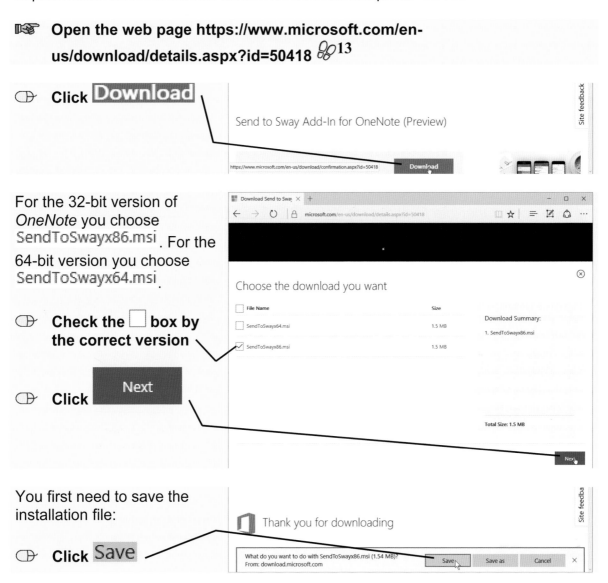

☞ **Click** Download

For the 32-bit version of *OneNote* you choose SendToSwayx86.msi. For the 64-bit version you choose SendToSwayx64.msi.

☞ **Check the ☐ box by the correct version**

☞ **Click** Next

You first need to save the installation file:

☞ **Click** Save

Then you can run the installation:

⊕ **Click** Run

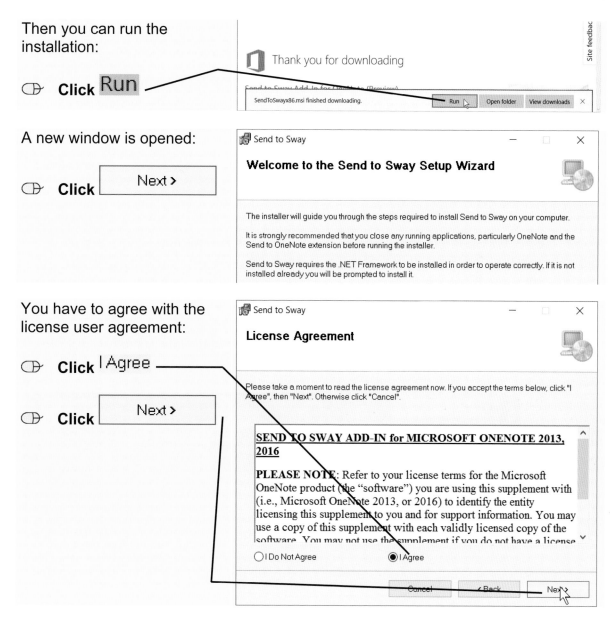

A new window is opened:

⊕ **Click** Next >

You have to agree with the license user agreement:

⊕ **Click** I Agree

⊕ **Click** Next >

You can specify whether just you or also other users of the computer are allowed to use *Send to Sway*. In this example, the option for everyone is chosen:

⊕ **Click** Everyone

⊕ **Click** Next >

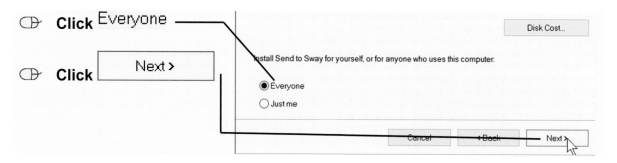

🖱️ **Click**

Your screen may turn dark, and you will need to give permission before continuing:

☞ **Give permission to continue**

Once the installation is complete.

🖱️ **Click** [Close]

If you have downloaded the plug-in, you can now perform the following actions. In this example, you can see how a *Sway* of a page created in *OneNote* is made:

☞ **Open *OneNote* 🦶¹**

☞ **Open the *Lamborghini* notebook from the *Exercise files OneNote* folder 🦶11**

Send To

🖱️ **Click** Sway

A *Sway* is made from the current page.

OneNote is getting ready to create a *Sway*. You still must login with your *Microsoft* account:

🖱️ **Click** [Sign In]

⌨ **Type your email address** ─────

🖱 **Click** Next

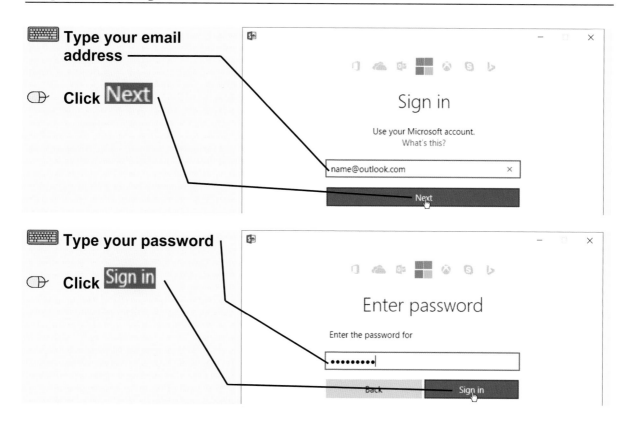

⌨ **Type your password**

🖱 **Click** Sign in

Next you see the following window:

The title of the page is automatically copied and is also used as the title of the *Sway*: ─────

You can change the title, if you want:

To continue:

🖱 **Click** Sway it

After converting the page, the web address (URL) is shown. You can view the *Sway* in an Internet browser:

You may need to login again with your *Microsoft* account if you want to continue:

☞ **If necessary, log in with your *Microsoft* account** 🐾**62**

The *Sway* presentation opens. There are two modes in *Sway*. In the first, the storyline, adjustments to *Sway* can still be made. In the second, you can take a preview of the presentation as others will see it.

Below, you first see the storyline:

Here you can adjust the presentation, if needed:

Sway works with so-called cards. Somewhat similar to *PowerPoint's* slides, you can insert an image, video, tweet, chart, text, etcetera to a card:

You can change the design:

You can choose which way your *Sway* goes: up and down or left to right:

You can let *Sway* create a new layout or 'flavor' for you:

To view the *Sway* as others will see it:

☞ **Click** Preview

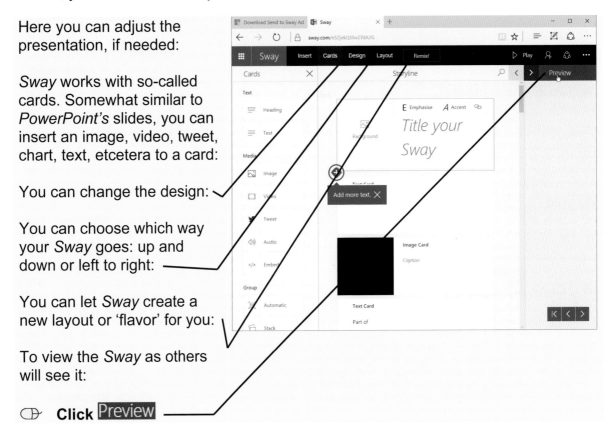

You now see the result:

If you want to edit the *Sway* even further, click Storyline:

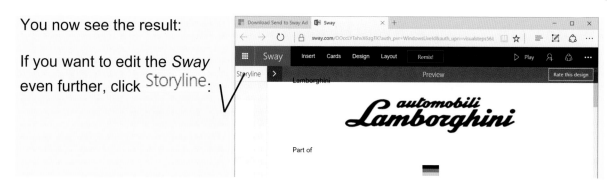

💡 **Tip**
Video on the book's website
On the book's website **www.visualsteps.com/onenote2016** you will find the official instructional video for *Sway*, which I created for *Microsoft*.

You can set up *Email to OneNote* in such a way that it allows you to send an email to me@onenote.com. From there it is saved to your *Quick Notes* section and the content can be added as pages to your notebook. This comes in handy for example, if you quickly want to add something to a notebook via your smartphone.

☞ **Open the website https://www.onenote.com/emailtoonenote** ¹³

↪ **Click**
Set up email to OneNo

For using *E-mail to OneNote* you need to register with your *Microsoft* account:

↪ **Click**
Sign in with a Microsoft acc

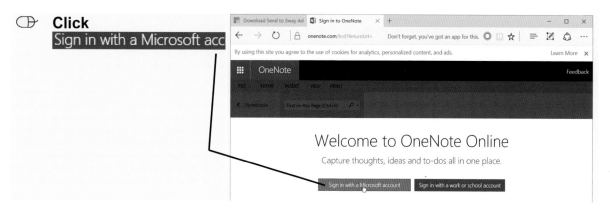

☞ **If necessary, log in with your *Microsoft* account** ✇**62**

Now the email address is associated with this task: ⎯⎯

☞ **Click** Default Location

Now you can choose the notebook, section and in some cases the pages you want to integrate with the content of the emails:

If you send an email from the associated email address to me@onenote.com, it can be placed within the chosen page.

If you want to place the content of your email to another section than the standard installed section, you can insert the 'at' symbol @ and the name of the section at the end of the chapter: ⎯⎯

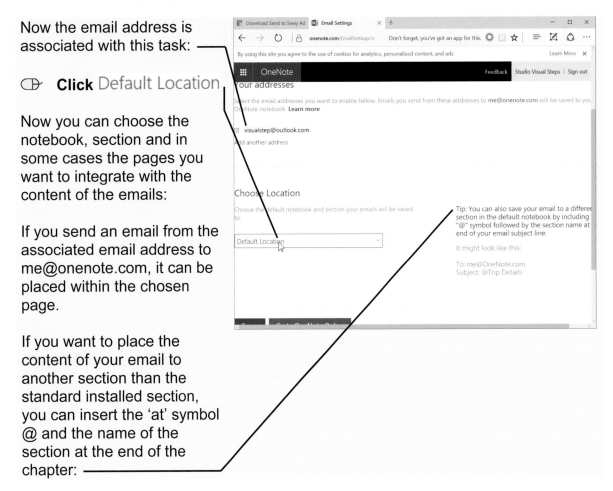

In this chapter you learned about several plug-ins or add-ins for *OneNote*. In the next chapter, two more plug-ins will be addressed, mostly interesting for educational purposes: *Learning tools* and *Class notebook*.

☞ **Close all windows** ✇**10**

7.4 Exercises

The following exercises will help you master what you have just learned. Have you forgotten how to perform a certain action? The number next to the footsteps tells you where to look it up at the end of the book in the appendix *How Do I Do That Again?*

Exercise 1: Digitizing a Document

In this exercise you will digitize a page from a newspaper or magazine.

☞ Open *OneNote*. 🦶1

☞ Open the *Scan* notebook from the *Exercise files OneNote* folder. 🦶11

☞ Share this notebook on *OneDrive*. 🦶63

☞ Use *Office Lens* to scan a page from a newspaper or magazine of your choice and export the scan to the *Scan* notebook. 🦶64

☞ Synchronize the notebook in *OneNote*. 🦶55

☞ Open the page you just made. 🦶16

☞ Copy the text from the image and paste this text in the *Newspaper* page. 🦶37

☞ Close *OneNote*. 🦶10

7.5 Background Information

Glossary

Gem	This plug-in extends *OneNote* with many extra features. *Gem* offers at least five new tabs. It is offered for a free, thirty-day trial. After that period, the app will need to be purchased.
Macro	Macros allow you to automate tasks. A macro is a saved sequence of commands, actions or keystrokes that can be stored and run later on whenever you need to perform the same task.
Office Lens	This app can be installed on your smartphone or tablet. It enables you to scan documents and straighten them. Then they can be placed into *OneNote*.
OneTastic	This add-in gives you the option to crop photos. You can also use it to create, run and download macros.
Plug-in application	Also known as an app, extension, add-in, add-on or plug-in. Usually a small application that extends a program with extra features.
Sway	Free service for making and sharing online presentations. With the *Email to OneNote* feature, you can quickly add content to *OneNote* notebooks by email.
WordPress	A free and open source Content Management System (CMS) for building websites. A CMS is a system with which you can build websites online without having to buy extra software.

Source: OneNote help function, Wikipedia

7.6 Tips

 Tip

Exporting slides from PowerPoint to OneNote
It is also possible to export slides from a *PowerPoint* presentation to *OneNote*. You start from a presentation already opened in *PowerPoint*:

☞ **Click** File

☞ **Click** Print

☞ **By** Printer**, select**
Send To OneNote 2016

☞ **Click**

☞ **By the desired notebook, click** ⊞

☞ **Click the desired section**

☞ **Click** OK

The slides are being exported to *OneNote* and will be placed there on separate pages:

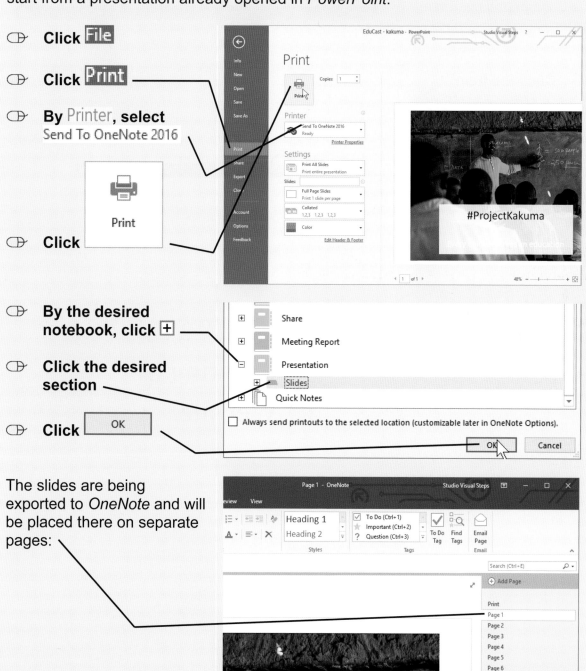

Tip

Exporting Office Lens to Word

When you export a photo from *Office Lens* to *Word*, it will end up in *OneDrive*. You can edit the document directly in *OneDrive*:

In *OneDrive* you can trace the document back to the folder *Files > Documents > Office Lens*:

☞ **Click the item**

You can edit the document directly in *Word Online*:

If you want to edit the file in *Word*:

☞ **Click EDIT IN WORD**

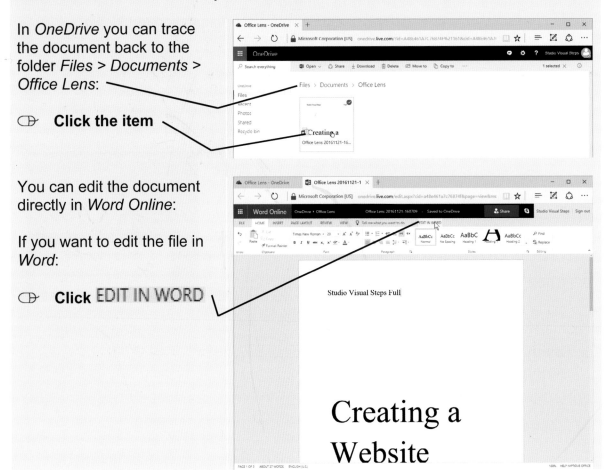

8. OneNote for Teachers

OneNote is often used in education. Teachers use it for various tasks, such as creating digital handbooks, for tests and study related tasks, as a replacement for the whiteboard, as an aid for a dyslectic student, for group collaboration and much more.

This chapter will address a number of interesting applications. Even if you are not a teacher, this will hopefully inspire you.

In this chapter you learn how to:

- use *OneNote* as replacement for the whiteboard;
- use *OneNote* as a tool for students to reflect, participate and collaborate;
- use *OneNote* as a tool for processing information;
- use *OneNote* as a presentation tool;
- use *Classroom notebook* for evaluation and giving feedback on tests;
- install and use the *Learning tools* plug-in application;
- combine *Learning tools* and *Office Lens*;
- convert paper documents to digital text, which can then be read aloud;
- make use of the benefits of a digital course.

8.1 Digital Board

For decades, a chalkboard was present in every classroom. The downside of the chalk board is that every time the board was cleaned, all the information was lost. Nowadays, chalk is also becoming more inconvenient in a class using computers or tablets as the dust can penetrate keyboards and screens, making them harder to work with. *OneNote* can be used as replacement for the chalkboard. A digital pen can be used to record the information in the notebook. Some advantages are:

- the information does not disappear but is saved;
- the notebook can be shared with everyone;
- the information is reusable for future classes;
- you can draw in different colors, on photos and you can delete inks;
- you can zoom in and out;
- the board schedule can be printed.

For example, a sketch of the water cycle on a chalkboard:

And here the same sketch in *OneNote*:

First the image was inserted, then names and pointers were added with a digital pen:

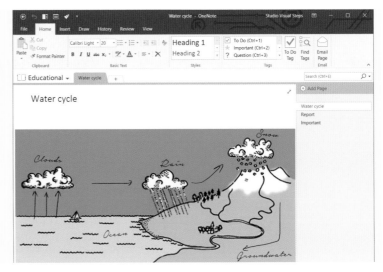

Viewing the image becomes even easier by switching to full screen mode in *OneNote*:

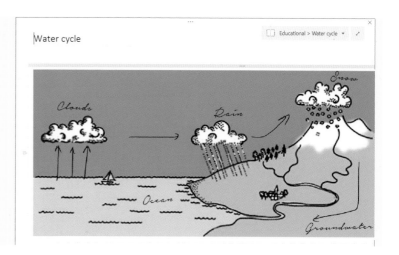

This page can be reused in subsequent school years. The colors are clearer than chalk and, if necessary, the result can be printed. The *OneNote* page can also be shared with the students. You can even make a case that *OneNote* combined with a projector, can replace an expensive digital board.

8.2 Reflection, Participation and Collaboration

Participation during class stimulates students and helps them to build their knowledge and is very important when working in groups. Research has shown that as students work together solving problems, they discover new things about themselves. Knowledge that is constructed by a student himself will be easier to remember and put to use than knowledge that is taught in a less interactive way. The students will be more motivated too. This is the basis of social constructivism.

You can create a *OneNote* notebook in which students can brainstorm in class. They can contribute ideas, questions, comments, wishes and their own experiences and write about them in a class notebook.

Example: In a lesson, the student learns how to publish a website on the Internet. Perhaps the students have done this before. You can ask them what web hosting they were using and what their experiences were. In a shared notebook all students can write down their experiences with a digital pen.

An example:

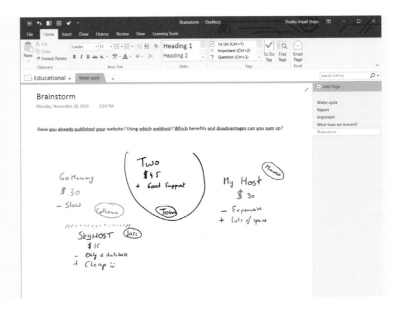

A digital pen has value when you are brainstorming like this. Psychologists Pam Mueller and Daniel Oppenheimer researched taking notes on laptops. They found that taking notes with a pen (handwriting) is better than typing text. Writing with the pen generates more thinking. One thinks more about individual words, there is no spelling correction and from a general point of view, the student starts thinking more critically. When he writes, the brain is going to make a bigger commitment (connection) with the material, then when it is typed.

It would be unfortunate if knowledge disappears from the minds of students, only to briefly return during an exam period. Who has not had the experience of sitting down to do a quiz and suddenly realizes that material studied earlier in the year has not 'sunk in' and is now completely lost? During the learning process, it is necessary for students to reflect on this.

Example: As a teacher you can create a notebook in *OneNote*, and share it with the students; during every lesson two different students record in this notebook what they learned that day. This way students learn working together, learn to reflect and put in their own words what they learned that day. They may even give suggestions or pointers to other classmates.

For example:

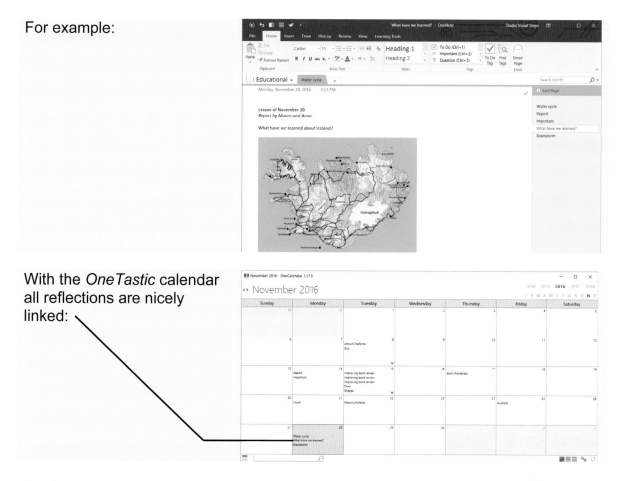

With the *OneTastic* calendar all reflections are nicely linked:

Students can also use *OneNote* individually for keeping track of their notes, assignments and progress. They can create a portfolio and put this online.

You can also provide groups of students with a separate page, section or notebook in which they can work together and go exploring.

Example: You want to teach about twenty different trees in one lesson. You divide your class into five groups. Each group must study four different trees: their leaves, medicinal properties, fruit and if applicable how the wood is used. The groups will each delve into their four trees. They will probably remember these years later, because they were actively engaged in building their knowledge. They learned how to search for and process information themselves. During the next class each group presents their four trees to their classmates.

For example:

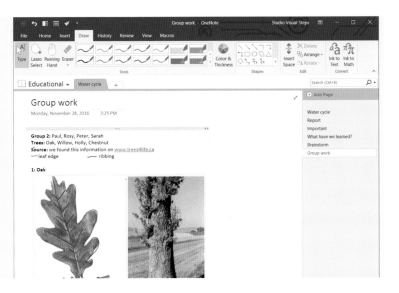

Using *OneNote* may also be a way to give parents insight into what their children are doing. It may even be a means of communication between teacher and parents, allowing the parents to get a better insight into the progress of their children. In the example below the teacher created a notebook for each student and which was then shared with the parents periodically. They could then follow their child's progress and behavior on the basis of the teacher's notes. Parents can also ask questions this way.

The notebook with the teacher's remarks:

Another possibility with collaboration is by using *OneNote* as a means of support and communication between colleagues. It is a great tool for making meeting reports. Teachers can also use *OneNote* to share ideas, tests and other course components with each other.

8.3 Processing Information

The tag function in *OneNote* can be very interesting for processing information. Students often have to read a text and then discuss it. Or make a report. By creating new tags and linking them to pieces of text, a summary can be created quite easily, with links to the various pieces of text.

☞ **Open *OneNote* 🦶¹**

☞ **Open the *Educational* notebook from the *Exercise files OneNote* folder 🦶11**

☞ **Open the page *Report* 🦶16**

You will practice assigning tags to a few sections in the text:

⌨ **Click to the left of the word 'global'**

⌨ **Press** ⏎ **Enter**

⌨ **By** Tags **, click** ▾

⌨ **Click** ⭐ **Important**

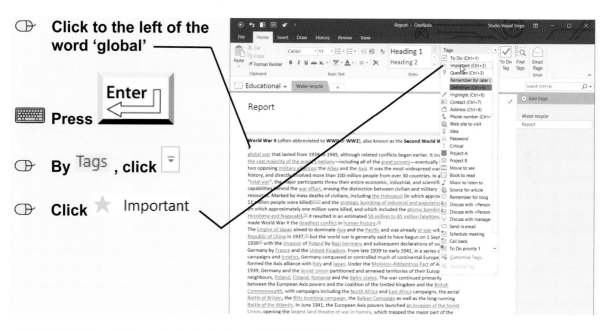

☞ **Put the following texts on a new line: 'In a state …' and 'The war …'**

☞ **Also add an important tag to the left of: 'In a state…' and 'The Empire of Japan …'**

Now you can make a summary page:

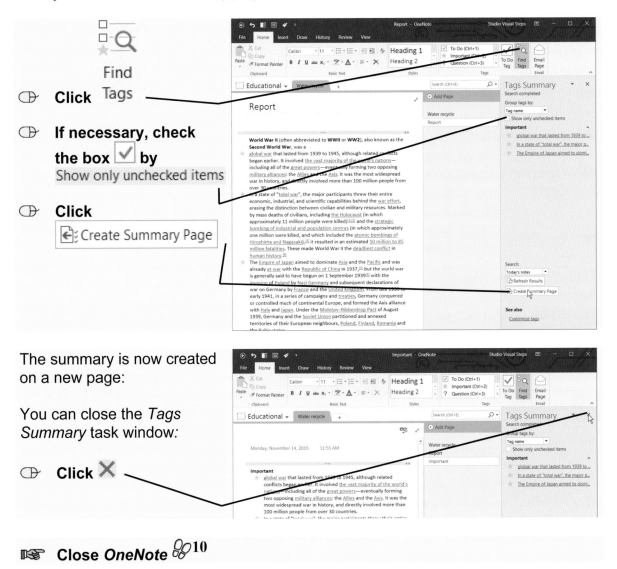

Click Find Tags

If necessary, check the box ☑ by Show only unchecked items

Click Create Summary Page

The summary is now created on a new page:

You can close the *Tags Summary* task window:

Click ✕

☞ **Close OneNote** ⬤⬤ 10

8.4 Presentation Tool

PowerPoint, *Sway* or *Prezi* are widely used to make presentations. *PowerPoint*, you probably know from the *Office* suite. *Sway* (discussed in *section 7.3 Other plug-ins*) and *Prezi* are web-based programs for creating presentations in an Internet browser. *OneNote* can also be used for making presentations.

An empty page in *OneNote* will be the start for the presentation and also the page on which to place the slides. Here is a list of some of the options available:

- In *OneNote* you can easily navigate from top to bottom and from left to right.
- With digital ink you can draw arrows between the various slides for pointing to the desired order.
- It is easy to place the slides in a different order. Something to consider if you change your mind at the last moment.
- It is possible to put extra sources in the side margin.
- You can share the presentation via a web address (URL) with your audience so they are able to view the presentation as well.
- You can specify a link, allowing the audience to place questions in your presentation while you are presenting it. This can be done between the slides or on a separate page. With the QR-code your public has easy access to the presentation.
- If you present the page full screen, no one will even notice that you are using *OneNote* to present it.
- If you have a tablet, you can swipe through the presentation, zoom in on details, zoom out for a larger view and make notes with a digital pen to emphasize certain details.
- If you make a connection with the projector via *Miracast*, you can also freely move through the audience. A *Miracast* is a small device you can connect to your computer, enabling you to make a wireless connection to a TV or projector. Other devices like *Miracast* with similar options are obtainable as well.

The author used the next presentation when he presented *OneNote* to a group of teachers at *Microsoft's* head office.

Photos and text are inserted:

A QR code and link which allows the public to view the presentation:

Arrows for establishing the order of the slides:

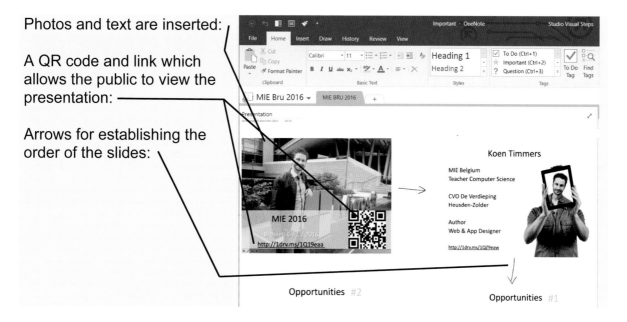

You can zoom in and show the presentation per slide:

Also you can show the presentation full screen; this way no one can see you are using *OneNote*:

By zooming out you can show your public the entire presentation. This way they can get a feel for the overall length of the presentation:

You can place extra sources and information in the side margin for those people who would like to know more. These extra sources can be text, links, photos, audio, video and more:

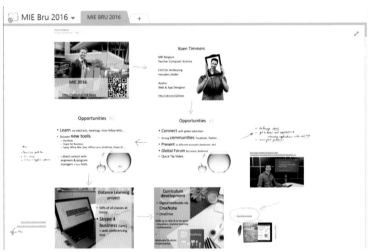

Make an extra page for your public to ask questions or give remarks. This will make your presentation more dynamic and your public more active:

By placing these tags you can check off the questions that have been answered. This not only gives you a quick overview of your feedback, it helps you to stay more organized as well:

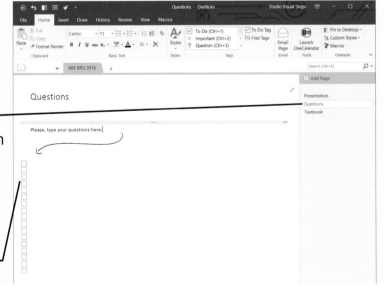

8.5 Evaluation and Feedback

Tests are often given for evaluation purposes. Still, most of the time they are handed out on paper and completed on paper as well, and after that a lot of checking and correction work awaits. This paper mountain is not very eco-friendly. Using *OneNote Class Notebook*, it is possible to spread out a *OneNote* page to your students. Your students will all get their own copy in which they have to fill in their answers and if applicable their notes or explanations. Then, all copies are collected to a central point and made accessible to the teacher. After that, the teacher can give feedback, which is immediately visible to the students.

OneNote Class Notebook is only visible if the school has a subscription for an *Office 365* environment and each student has their own school email address. For this reason, you may not be able to test this plug-in yourself. On this website you can check whether your school is using the correct version of *Office 365*: https://products.office.com/en-us/student/office-in-education?tab=teachers. If that is the case, all teachers and students from the school will be able to use a free *Office 365* account.

You can download the plug-in application from the website
https://www.onenote.com/classnotebook

After installation, *OneNote*
will show a new *Class*
Notebook tab: ────

 Please note:
The following steps can only be performed if your school or other facility has the appropriate subscription to *Office 365*.

☞ **Open *OneNote*** [1]

☞ **Open the notebook *Educational* from the *Exercise files OneNote* folder**
[11]

☞ **Open the page *Report*** [16]

You can create class notebooks (also known as lesson notebooks) and add and remove teachers and students. In the following steps you can use your own files and information if you want:

☞ **If necessary, click the** Class Notebook **tab**

☞ **Click** Create Class Notebook

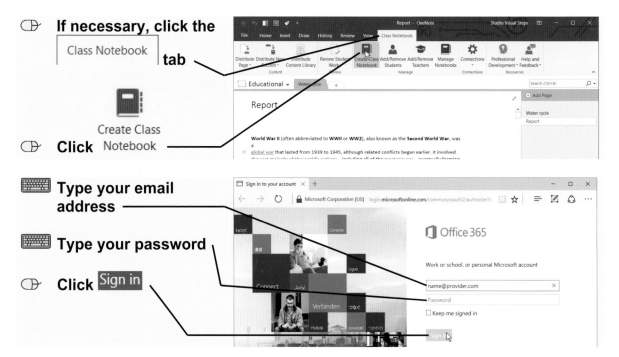

⌨ **Type your email address**

⌨ **Type your password**

☞ **Click** Sign in

You see the following window:

⌨ **Type the desired name in the text box**

☞ **Click** Next

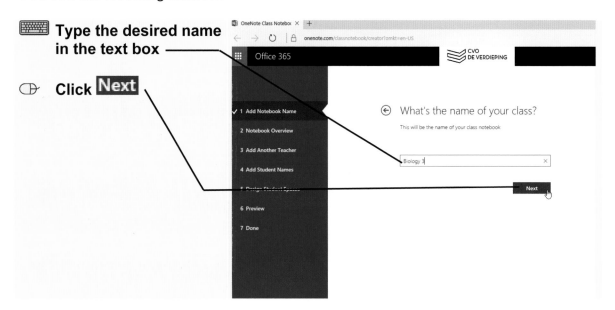

You receive a confirmation that the class notebook has been made. You can continue:

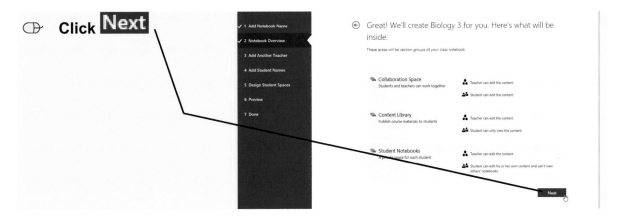

You can add another teacher. As the creator of this notebook, you are always included. You can continue:

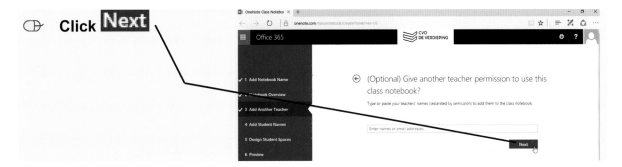

Now you can add the names of the students:

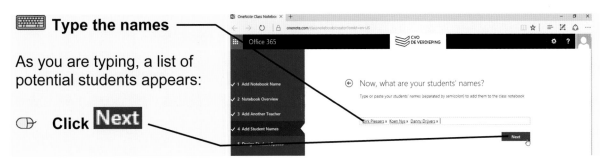

You now will see an overview of what the class notebook will contain. There are four standard sections, but you can add more later on.

This is not needed now:

Click Next

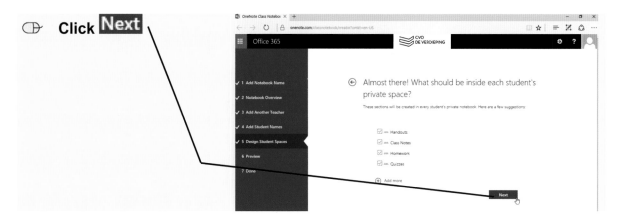

The next window is informative and shows you what the class notebook will look like.

Click Create

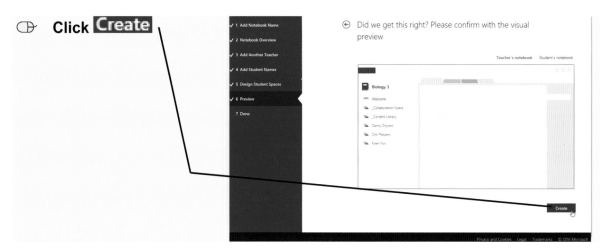

You are finished now and ready to return to *OneNote*:

Click
Open in OneNote

The class notebook appears in *OneNote*:

Student notebook, a notebook that can only be viewed by the student involved:

Content library, a notebook which is readable for each student. The teacher can use this notebook for sharing course material:

Space for collaboration, which can be viewed and edited by each student:

You can take a look at the student notebook:

⊕ **Click**

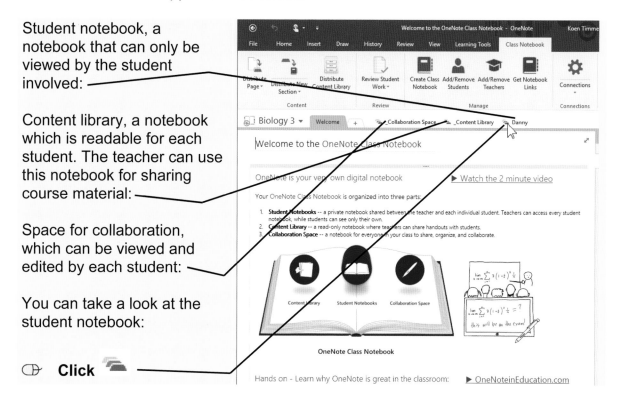

Here you see the personal notebook of just one student.

Teachers can send homework, tests, quizzes and handouts to their students. These can only be edited by just one student:

The student can also maintain his own notes:

You can try this for yourself:

⊕ **Click** Quizzes

⌨ **Type some text**

To return to the overview:

⊕ **Click** 5

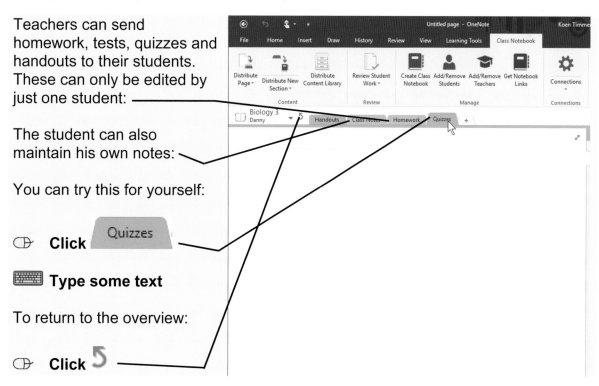

You can prevent a lot of work by sending an existing test to each student all at once:

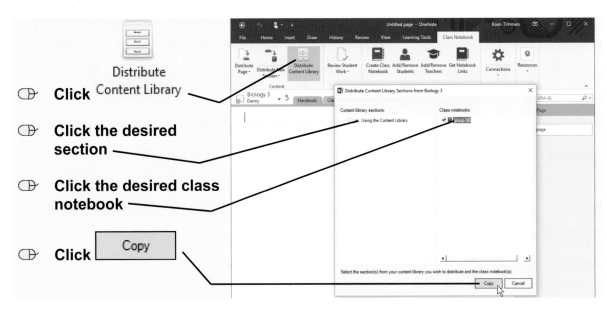

Click **Content Library**

Click **the desired section**

Click **the desired class notebook**

Click **Copy**

This means you only need to create a test, note or homework assignment one time. You can distribute it to your students all in one go:

☞ **Create a new page** ❧⁶

Click **Distribute Page** ▾

Click **Quizzes**

If necessary, you can also exclude students by deleting the check ✔ by their names:

To continue:

Click **Copy**

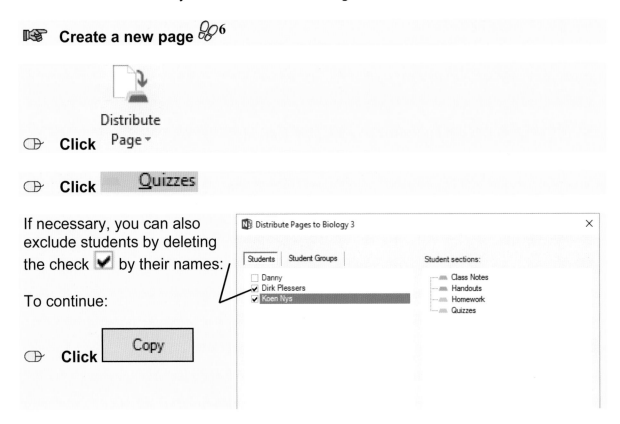

As a teacher you can correct tests or quizzes very quickly:

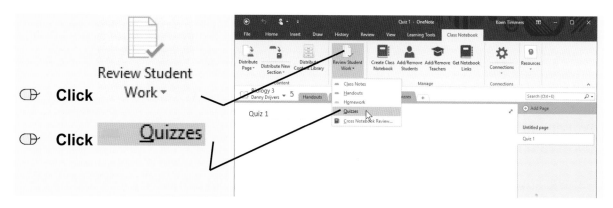

👆 **Click** Review Student Work ▾

👆 **Click** Quizzes

A new window appears. This is where you can see the students who received a test:

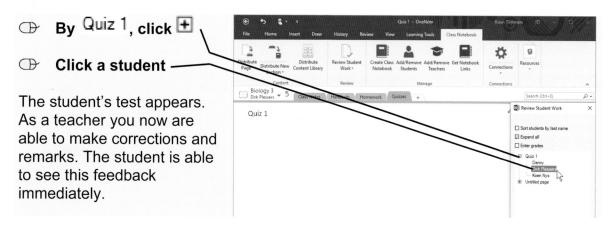

👆 **By** Quiz 1, **click** ➕

👆 **Click a student**

The student's test appears. As a teacher you now are able to make corrections and remarks. The student is able to see this feedback immediately.

You can always add more students or teachers to the class notebook:

This can be done by clicking

Add/Remove Students . It works the same way as previously discussed:

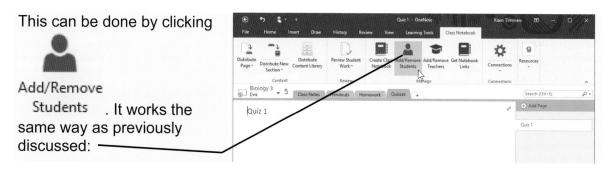

You have now had a glimpse of the primary components of the *Class Notebook* plug-in application.

👉 **Close** *OneNote* 10

8.6 From Paper, to Digital Text, to Voice

The free plug-in *Learning Tools*, was developed specifically for educational purposes, in particular to make things easier for dyslexic students. *Learning Tools* offers the following features:
• dictation: voice is converted into editable text;
• text read: text is converted into voice;
• presenting text more clearly for students with different abilities;
• phrases are automatically recognized in text.

Dyslexic students often have trouble with word order. They can also easily skip a line of text without noticing it. *Learning tools* offers the option to darken the background and enlarge the distance between the text lines and the words.

The *Learning tools* plug-in application can be downloaded for free from http://www.onenote.com/learningtools

☞ **Open the web page www.onenote.com/learningtools** 👣**13**

You can install the plug-in:

First you save the file and then allow the installation to run:

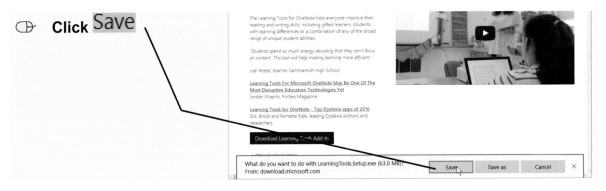

⊕ **Click** Run

You have to agree with the license user agreement in the next window:

⊕ **Check the box** ☐ **by** I agree to the license terms and conditions

⊕ **Click**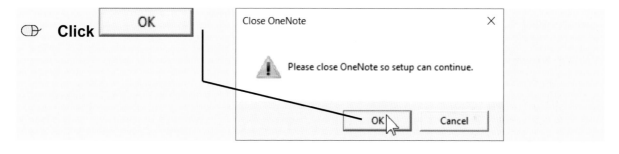

Your screen may go dark and you will need to give permission in order to continue:

☞ **If necessary, give permission to continue**

OneNote must be closed during installation. If *OneNote* is still open:

⊕ **Click** OK

Close OneNote ✕

⚠ Please close OneNote so setup can continue.

OK   Cancel

☞ **Close** *OneNote* ⚆⚆ **10**

Your computer needs to be restarted before you can start using *Learning tools*:

☞ **Close all opened windows** ⚆⚆ **10**

⊕ **Click**
Launch OneNote

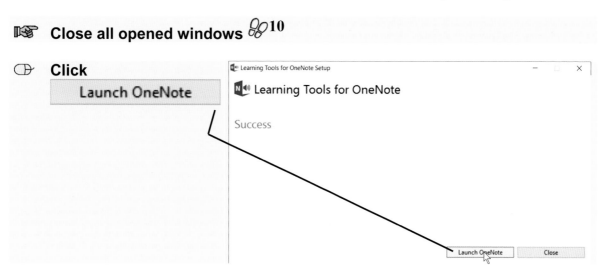

◀ Learning Tools for OneNote Setup   — ☐ ✕

N Learning Tools for OneNote

Success

Launch OneNote   Close

☞ **If necessary, open *OneNote* 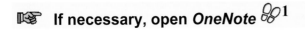1**

☞ **Open the notebook *Extension* (stored in *OneDrive*) ⛾65**

You see the new tab *Learning tools*:

◔ **If necessary, click the**

Learning Tools **tab**

When you combine *Learning tools* with *Office Lens*, you are able to move from paper to digital text to voice. As an example, scan a paper document with some text for example a poem. The poem used here can be printed from the website of this book.

☞ **Make the scan and export it to the *Extension* notebook, in the section *Scans* in *OneNote* and name the page *Poem* ⛾64**

☞ **Synchronize the notebook in *OneNote* ⛾55**

You will see the scan on a new page. It is now an image:

◔ **Click Poem**

You can copy the text from the image and paste it, thereby replacing the image:

☞ **Copy the text from the image and paste it below the image ⛾37**

☞ **Delete the image ⛾38**

You now have editable text and can begin to work with *Learning tools*:

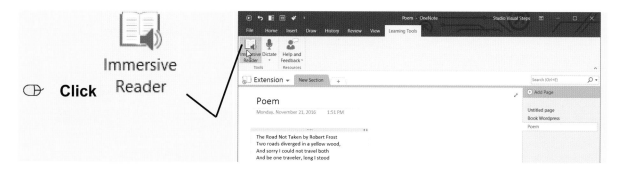

⊕ **Click** Immersive Reader

A new window appears with the text enlarged:

The text is now easier to read, especially for a dyslexic student.

To have the text be read aloud:

⊕ **Click** ▶

You can now hear the text, provided the sound on your computer or speakers is on.

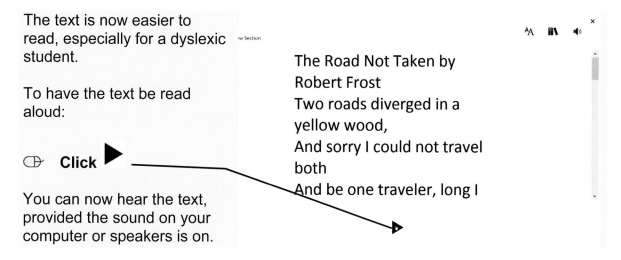

Each word is highlighted the moment it is read:

To stop the text being read:

⊕ **Click** ❚❚

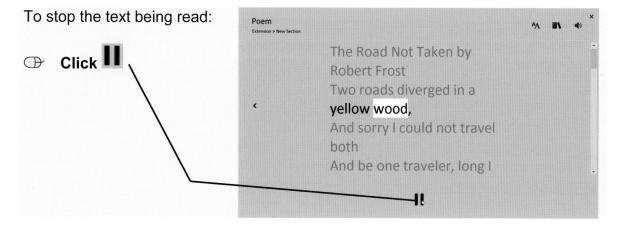

Learning tools can also highlight certain parts of a sentence:

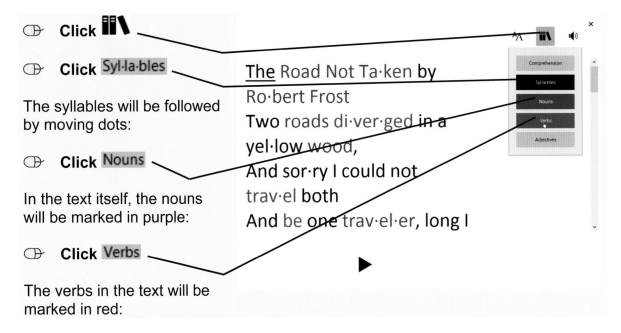

- Click 📚

- Click Syl·la·bles

The syllables will be followed by moving dots:

- Click Nouns

In the text itself, the nouns will be marked in purple:

- Click Verbs

The verbs in the text will be marked in red:

You can take a look at other settings:

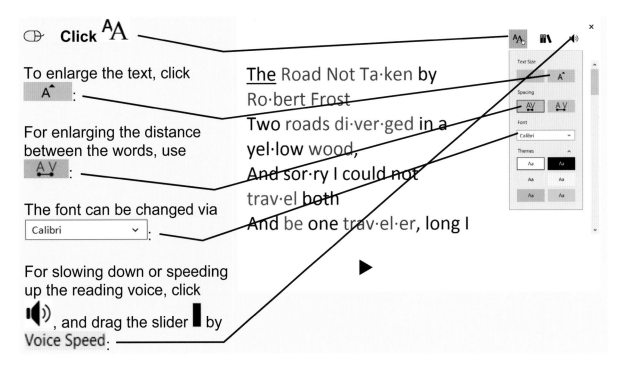

- Click ᴬA

To enlarge the text, click A⌃ :

For enlarging the distance between the words, use A V :

The font can be changed via Calibri ⌄ :

For slowing down or speeding up the reading voice, click 🔊 , and drag the slider ▌ by Voice Speed.

Research has shown that dyslexic students can improve their reading when the letters are shown against a dark background:

To switch the background color to black:

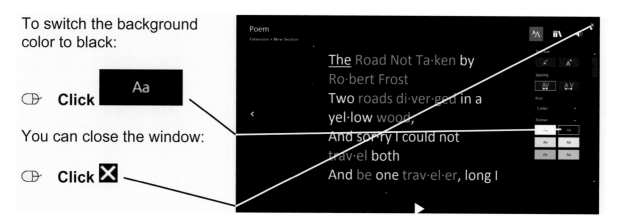

⊕ **Click**

You can close the window:

⊕ **Click** ✖

You can also make a dictation. *Learning tools* will then convert your voice into editable text. You will need a microphone for that, and one that is connected to your computer:

⊕ **Click below the text**

⊕ **Click** 🎤

A new window may open that requires you to login with your *Microsoft* account:

☞ **Log in with your *Microsoft* account** 𝒪𝒪62

The button has changed to 🎤

Dictate.

☞ **Speak some text, for instance "I like learning tools"**

To stop the recording:

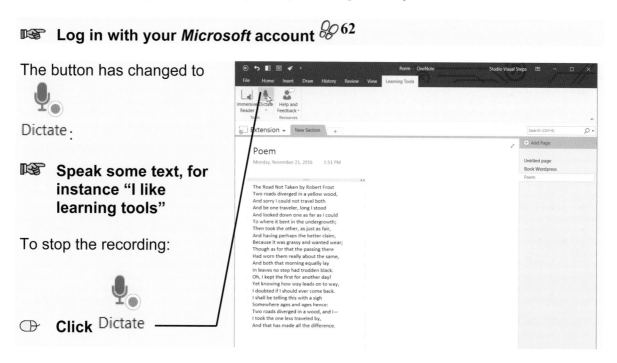

⊕ **Click** Dictate

Learning tools will display the spoken sentence below the existing text:

You can see the sentence:

In this section you have gotten acquainted with *Learning tools*. This plug-in application has specific advantages for dyslexic students or others with different abilities, but it is also interesting for anyone wanting to convert text to voice or voice to text.

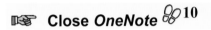 **Close** *OneNote* ᵔᵔ **10**

8.7 Digital Handbooks

Handbooks, course curriculums and course syllabi can tend to be rather dull. To save costs they are often printed in black and white. They may even contain errors sometimes. Or a teacher may want to add extra information regarding a certain lesson. In that case, a number of separate paper pages need to be created. After a while these types of documents can become outdated. A digital version of a handbook or other similar documents allows a teacher to maintain the documents and add pertinent information when needed, even during a lesson.

Via *OneNote* you can create digital handbooks and other course documents. This has many advantages:

- The document is always 100% up-to-date and to-the-point.
- The document can be shared easily.
- Information can easily be retrieved with the search and tag functions.
- Students may be allowed to participate and add their own notes in a separate page. This creates a collaborative situation where everyone can learn from each other.
- The handbook is always accessible (in the cloud for example).
- Students can access the handbook by smartphone, tablet, laptop or computer.
- Hyperlinks can easily link pages together, thus facilitating the finding of information; it makes the handbook almost look like a website.
- The handbook is eco-friendly.
- Via *Office Lens* it is also easy to digitize paper documents and combine them into a digital handbook. Note the copyright, where applicable.

Here you see an example of a digital handbook:

In the section *Course content*,
the digital course is
explained. The many pages
keep the chapters separated:

The content consists of text,
images, links and sketches:

The search function allows
you to jump to a specific topic
quickly and easily:

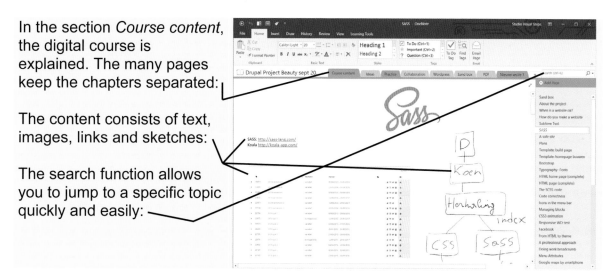

The digital course offers ample room for collaboration, even stimulates it:

In the *Collaboration* section,
students are free to make
notes on their own personal
page. Students learn from
each other and subsequently
the teacher from the students:

Here you see the notes of a
student named Stephan:

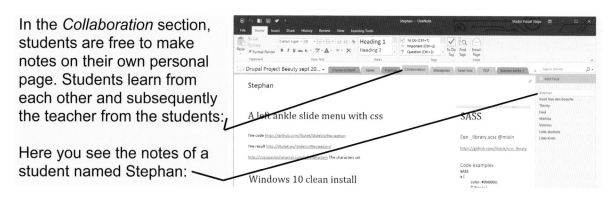

Not only is there space for the course material itself, but also for ideas, questions,
comments and requests:

In the *Ideas* section a number
of interesting additions have
been suggested for the
lessons:

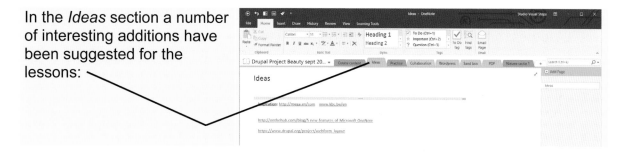

In this section, you have learned about the benefits of digital handbooks and other course documents and the importance of collaboration in contemporary education. In other sections of this chapter, you have seen that *OneNote* can be of great use in education. The program lends itself well as a replacement for the classic chalkboard, printed handbooks, presentations and even allows the digitization of paper documents. Thanks to the two plug-in applications *Learning tools* and *Class Notebook* you can go even a step further. You can support dyslexic students in a better way, distribute and correct homework more efficiently and move from speech to text and vice versa.

You have now reached the end of the book. In this book you have acquainted yourself with the many useful features of *OneNote*. I hope these options have inspired you and I hope as well that you will use *OneNote* in the future with much satisfaction.

8.8 Visual Steps Website and Newsletter

By now we hope you have noticed that the Visual Steps method is an excellent method for quickly and efficiently learning more about computers, tablets, other devices and software applications. All books published by Visual Steps use this same method.

In various series, we have published a large number of books on a wide variety of topics including *Windows*, *MacOS*, the iPad, iPhone, Samsung Galaxy Tab, photo editing and many other topics.

On the **www.visualsteps.com** website you will find a full product summary by clicking the blue *Catalog* button. For each book there is an extensive description, the full table of contents and a sample chapter (PDF file). In this way, you can quickly determine if a specific title will meet your expectations. You can order a book directly online from this website or other online book retailers. All titles are also available in bookstores in the USA, Canada, United Kingdom, Australia and New Zealand.

Furthermore, the website offers many extras, among other things:
- free computer guides and booklets (PDF files) covering all sorts of subjects;
- frequently asked questions and their answers;
- information on the free Computer Certificate that you can acquire at the certificate's website **www.ccforseniors.com**;
- a free email notification service: let's you know when a new book is published.

There is always more to learn. Visual Steps offers many other books on computer-related subjects. Each Visual Steps book has been written using the same step-by-step method with short, concise instructions and screen shots illustrating every step.

Would you like to be informed when a new Visual Steps title becomes available? Subscribe to the free Visual Steps newsletter (no strings attached) and you will receive this information in your inbox.

The Newsletter is sent approximately each month and includes information about
- the latest titles;
- supplemental information concerning titles previously released;
- new free computer booklets and guides;

When you subscribe to our Newsletter you will have direct access to the free booklets on the **www.visualsteps.com/info_downloads.php** web page.

8.9 Background information

Glossary

Class Notebook	With *OneNote Class Notebook*, it is possible to distribute a *OneNote* page to each of your students. And they all get their own copy where they can add their answers to the questions asked. All copies are then collected at a central point and made accessible to the teacher. Next, the teacher can give his feedback, and this is immediately visible to the students. *OneNote Class Notebook* is only possible if the school has an applicable subscription to an *Office 365* environment and each student has got his own school email address.
Digital board	A digital whiteboard is an interactive whiteboard with a graphical environment, provided by a computer. This allows information to be recorded, saved, displayed on the board in the form of pictures, videos and more.
Learning tools	The free plug-in application *Learning tools* has been developed specifically for educational purposes, and in particular to make things easier for dyslexic students. *Learning tools* is able to convert voice into editable text, convert text to voice, display text in a clear way and will automatically recognize phrases in a text. *OneNote Class Notebook* is only accessible if the school has a subscription for *Office 365* and each student has his own school email address.
Miracast	A *Miracast* is a small device that can be connected to your computer for making a wireless connection to a TV or projector. There are other devices available with similar options.
PowerPoint	A program for making presentations as part of the *Office* suite.
Prezi	A service for making online presentations.
QR-code	A code similar to a barcode, but designed in a square. When you scan a tablet or smartphone, this will provide you with information, such as a telephone number, email address, website or something similar.
Swipe	A movement with the fingers on the touchscreen of a tablet, smartphone, or a monitor/screen with touch features.

Source: OneNote help function, Wikipedia

Appendices

A. How Do I Do That Again?

The actions and exercises in this book are marked with footsteps: 🐾1
If you have forgotten how to do something, you can read how to do it again by finding the corresponding number in the list below.

🐾1 **Open *OneNote***
In Windows 10 and 8.1:

● Click ⊞

● Type: OneNote

● Click **OneNote** 2016 Desktop app

In Windows 7:

● Click ⊕

● Click ▶ All programs

● Click Microsoft Office

● Click Microsoft OneNote

🐾2 **Create a new notebook**
Storing on OneDrive:

● Click File

● Click New

● Click OneDrive - Personal

● By Notebook Name:, type the document name

● Click [Create Notebook]

For not sharing the notebook:

● Click Not now

🐾3 **Change section name**
● Right-click the desired tab

New Section 1

● Click Rename

● Type the desired name

● Press Enter

🐾4 **Create a new section**

● Click +

● Type the desired name

● Press Enter

🐾5 **Change the page name**
● Click above the date

● Type the desired name

● Press Enter

🐾6 **Create a new page**
● Click ⊕ Add Page

- Click above the date

- Type the desired name

- Press

7 Change page stacking order
- Place the pointer on the page name, press and hold down

- Drag the name upwards or downwards, then release the mouse button

8 Delete page
On the right-hand side of the window:
- Right-click the page

- Click ✗ <u>D</u>elete

9 Insert text
- Click the desired page

- Click somewhere in the white area of the page

- Type the desired text

10 Close window
- Click ✖

11 Open notebook from the *Exercise files OneNote* folder
- Click File

- Click Open

- Click ▢ This PC

- Click ↑ 🗁 Documents

- Click 🗎 Documents

- Double-click
  ▌ Exercise files OneNote

- Click the desired folder

To open the notebook:
- Click Open notebook

- Click Open

12 Select text
Lines:
- Place the pointer on the left side of the top line, press and hold down

- Drag the pointer down until all desired lines are selected

Word:
- Click a word two times

Text part:
- Drag the pressed-in mouse over the desired text

13 Open web page
- Click

- Click in the address bar

- Type the web address

- Press

14 Close task window
- Click ✗

15 Zoom
- Click the ▢ View tab

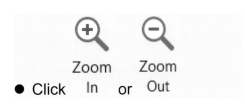

- Click   In   or   Out

Or:

- By , click ▼

- Click the desired size

16 Open page
On the right-hand side of the window:
- Click the page name

17 Apply styles
- Select the desired text **12**

- Click the | Home | tab

- By **Styles**, click the desired style

18 Apply text formatting
- Select the desired text **12**

- Click the desired formatting, for instance **B**, *I*, U̲ or **A** ▾

19 Add task tags
- Select the desired text **12**

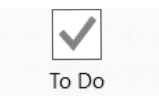

- Click   Tag

20 Link to another page
- Select the desired text **12**

- Right-click the selection

- Click 🌐 Link... (Ctrl+K)

- By the desired notebook, click ⊞

- By the desired section, click ⊞

- Click the desired page

- Click | OK |

21 Change page color
- Click the | View | tab

Page
- Click Color ▾

- Click the desired color

22 Add rule lines to a page
- Click the | View | tab

Rule
- Click Lines ▾

- Click the desired type of rule lines

23 Search tags
- Click the | Home | tab

- By **Search:**, select the option Today's notes (or the last period the notebook was worked on)

Find

- Click Tags

- By Group tags by: , select the
  option Tag name

For showing just the non-checked items:
- By Show only unchecked items ,
  check the box ☐

24 Create page with a page template

- Click the | Insert | tab

- Click

- Click the desired category

- Click the desired template

25 Dock page on desktop

- Click the | View | tab

Dock to
- Click Desktop

26 Copy and paste text

- Select the desired text ⚐ 12

- Click Ctrl + C

- Click the spot where you want
  to paste the text

- Click Ctrl + V

27 Turn off docking and return to Normal view

- Click ↗

28 Zoom to page width

- Click the | View | tab

- Click Page Width

29 Undo

- Click ↩

30 Program to the foreground
- Click the icon on the task bar,

  for instance

31 Screen shot

- Click the | Insert | tab

Screen
- Click Clipping

- Drag over the area you want
  to capture

32 Insert image

- Click the | Insert | tab

- Click Pictures

- Click the desired file

- Click

33 Insert image from website
- Right-click the picture

- Click Copy

- Right-click below the text

- Click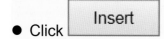

34 Insert online image
- Click the | Insert | tab

- Click Pictures

- Type a search term

- Press

(Enter key image)

- Click the desired image

- Click Insert

35 Move image
- Click the image

- Drag the image to the desired spot

36 Change stacking order
- Right-click the image

- Click ⌐└ Bring to Front or
  ☐ Send Backward

37 Copy text from image
- Right-click the image

- Click Copy Text from Picture

- Click the desired spot

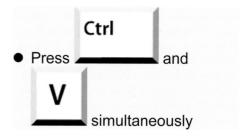

- Press **Ctrl** and **V** simultaneously

38 Delete image
- Click the image

- Press **Delete**

39 Open section
- Click the section's tab

40 Record audio clip
- Click the | Insert | tab

Record

- Click Audio

- Speak some text

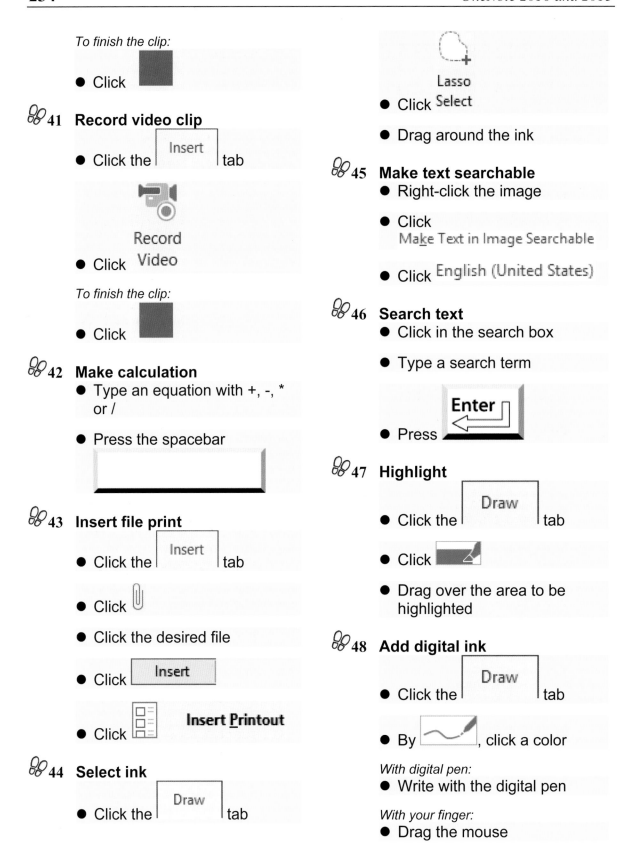

To finish the clip:

- Click

41 Record video clip

- Click the Insert tab

- Click Record Video

To finish the clip:

- Click

42 Make calculation

- Type an equation with +, -, * or /

- Press the spacebar

43 Insert file print

- Click the Insert tab

- Click

- Click the desired file

- Click Insert

- Click Insert Printout

44 Select ink

- Click the Draw tab

- Click Lasso Select

- Drag around the ink

45 Make text searchable

- Right-click the image

- Click Make Text in Image Searchable

- Click English (United States)

46 Search text

- Click in the search box

- Type a search term

- Press Enter

47 Highlight

- Click the Draw tab

- Click

- Drag over the area to be highlighted

48 Add digital ink

- Click the Draw tab

- By , click a color

With digital pen:
- Write with the digital pen

With your finger:
- Drag the mouse

49 Convert digital ink to text

- Click the Draw tab

- By Convert, click Ink to Text

50 Search pages in trash can

- Click the History tab

- Click Notebook Recycle Bin ▾

- Click ⬚ Notebook Recycle Bin

- Click the desired page

51 Delete pages in trash can

- Click the History tab

- Click Notebook Recycle Bin ▾

- Click ⬚ Empty Recycle Bin

- Click Delete

Return to the History tab:

- Click 🗑

52 Share and link notebook

- Click File

- Click Share

If the file is only saved on your computer:

- Click Move Notebook

- Click OK

If you also want to share with others:

- Click Can edit ▾

- Make the desired choice

If you want a link for sharing purposes:
- Click 🔗 Get a Sharing Link

- By Edit Link, click Create an edit link

- Right-click the link

- Click Copy

53 Edit notebook in web app

- Click ✏ Edit in Browser

54 Create a page with the web app

- Click Insert

- Click + Page

- Type the name of the page

55 Synchronize
- Right-click the notebook's name, for example ⬚ Meeting Report

- Click Sync This Notebook Now

56 Open *File Explorer*
On the task bar:

- Click

57 Translate
- Select the word to be translated

- Click the | Review | tab

Translate
- Click ▾

- Click
  Translate Selected Text
  Translate the selected text into a different language

- Click | Yes |

- By From and To , select the desired language

- Click | Insert |

To close the task window:
- Click ✕

58 Search synonym
- Select a word

- Click the tab | Review |

  📖
- Click Thesaurus

- Click the desired synonym

To close the task window:
- Click ✕

59 Research word
- Select a word

- Click Research

- By Translation , click ▾

- Click Bing

To close the task window:
- Click ✕

60 Export
- Click File

- Click Export

- Click 🖴 Section

- Click 📄 PDF (*.pdf)

- Click

  Export

- Select the desired folder

- Click | Save |

61 Print
- Click File

- Click Print

- Click

- If necessary, click the desired print settings

- Click Print...

- Click the desired printer

- Click Print...

📓 **62 Sign in with a *Microsoft* account**
- Type you email address

- Click Next

- Type your password

- Click Sign in

📓 **63 Share and link a notebook**
- Click File

- Click Share

If the notebook has been saved only on your computer:

- Click

- Click OK

📓 **64 Scan with *Office Lens***
- Open the app *Office Lens* on your smartphone

- Direct the camera to the document to be scanned

- Tap ⚫

- Tap Done

- Tap 📒 OneNote

- By Title, type a page title

- Tap Location

- Tap the desired notebook

- Tap the desired section

- Tap Save

📓 **65 Open notebook on *OneDrive***
- Click File

- Click Open

- Click
   OneDrive - Personal

- Click 📁 Documents

- Click the desired notebook

Or:
- Click the name of the current notebook

- Click the desired notebook

B. Downloading the Exercise Files

This appendix describes step by step how to download the exercise files from the website accompanying this book to your computer. Downloading means transferring files from the Internet to your own computer.

☞ **Open the web page www.visualsteps.com/onenote2016** &&13

You now see the website for this book. You can download the exercise files:

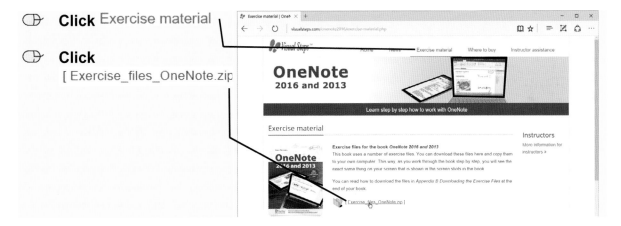

⊕ **Click** Exercise material

⊕ **Click**
[Exercise_files_OneNote.zip]

A bar or window appears. You can save the exercise files:

⊕ **Click** Save

Next, you open the folder where you have saved the exercise files:

⊕ **Click** Open folder

The *Exercise_files_OneNote.zip* folder is a compressed folder. This folder can be saved in your *Documents* folder:

In *Windows 10* and *8.1*:

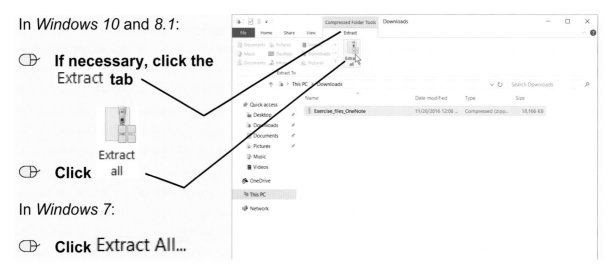

☞ **If necessary, click the** Extract **tab**

☞ **Click** Extract all

In *Windows 7*:

☞ **Click** Extract All...

The *Extract Compressed (Zipped) Folders* window is opened. Now you can browse to your *Documents* folder:

☞ **Click** Browse...

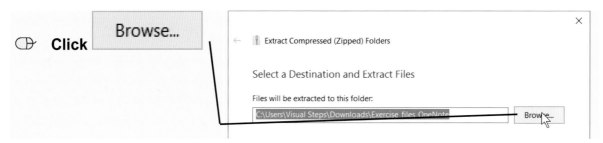

Create a new folder and name it *Exercise files OneNote*. You can save it in the *Documents* folder. In *Windows 10* you do the following. If you are working with *Windows 8.1* or *7,* continue on the next page.

☞ **Click** Documents

☞ **Click** New folder

⌨ **Type:** Exercise files OneNote

⌨ **Press** Enter

☞ **Click** Select Folder

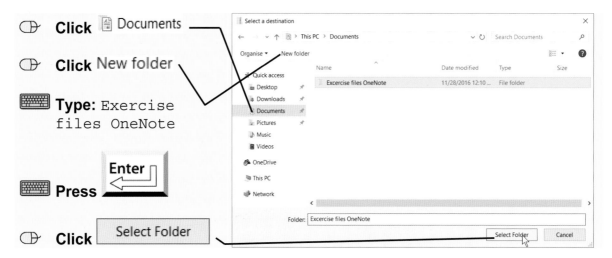

Windows 8.1 and 7

In *Windows 8.1* and *Windows 7* you see the window *Select target*:

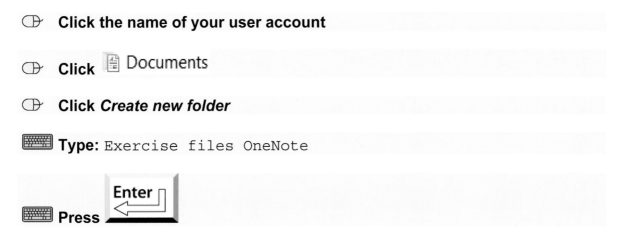

☞ **Click the name of your user account**

☞ **Click** 📄 Documents

☞ **Click *Create new folder***

⌨ **Type:** Exercise files OneNote

⌨ **Press** Enter ⏎

The new folder is now selected:

☞ **Click** OK

In all *Windows* versions:

In all versions of *Windows,* the files will now be extracted. The files are stored in the *Documents* folder:

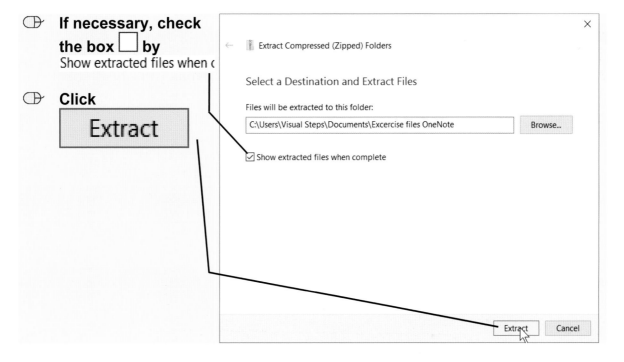

☞ **If necessary, check the box** ☐ **by**
Show extracted files when c

☞ **Click** Extract

Extract Compressed (Zipped) Folders

Select a Destination and Extract Files

Files will be extracted to this folder:

C:\Users\Visual Steps\Documents\Excercise files OneNote   Browse...

☑ Show extracted files when complete

Extract   Cancel

The files are being extracted. You can see the exercise files for this book:

You can close this window:

⊕ **Click** ✕

The compressed folder *Exercise_files_OneNote* is still stored in the *Downloads* folder. This window is still open. You can delete the compressed folder like this:

⊕ **Click the folder** ⎯⎯

Delete

▦ **Press** ⎯⎯

You may be asked to confirm this:

⊕ **If necessary, click** Yes

The compressed folder is now deleted.

☞ **Close the Internet browser** 👣10

The files are now saved to your computer. You can use them as you work through the steps in this book.

C. Index

Creating a Website with WordPress

For many people today, creating and updating a personal website has become a fun and enjoyable hobby. A website can be used to share information about your family history, business, favorite genre of music or even to post the latest news and event information for a local club or organization. Thanks to a variety of software and online services, creating a

website has never been easier. With the free, user-friendly WordPress software, you can make your own personal and professional website in no time at all. This practical how-to book, shows you step by step exactly what to do. You start off by choosing an attractive theme (template) with which to build your website. Then you fill the website with your own text, pictures, videos and hyperlinks. You can even include a photo gallery, a pulldown menu with links to other pages, or an online form enabling people to contact you. These are just a few of the things that can be added to your website. WordPress offers a wide variety of plugins and widgets that can easily add extra functionality to your website. By using this book and the software from WordPress, you will have everything you need to create your own website!

Author: Studio Visual Steps
ISBN 978 90 5905 422 6
Book type: Paperback, full color
Nr of pages: 264
Accompanying website:
www.visualsteps.com/wordpress

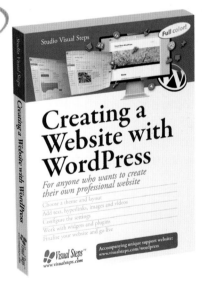

Learn how to:
- Choose a theme and layout
- Add text, hyperlinks, images and videos
- Configure the settings
- Work with widgets and plugins

Suitable for: Windows 10, 8.1, 7 and Mac.

Quick Introduction to the iPad and iPhone

Did you recently buy an iPad or iPhone, or have you owned one for a while and want to learn more about the device and the latest options and features? Then this book is the right one for you.

Apple's latest operating system iOS 10 has lots of new features which will make your iPhone or iPad an even more convenient device. For example, you can receive notifications from your apps, messages and news in the renewed Notification Center and respond to them directly right from there. The Messages app has been greatly enhanced as well. You can liven up your messages with animations, emojis and drawings.

This book shows you how to work with these new features and many standard apps on the iPad and iPhone are also covered. You will also learn how to quickly switch between apps, add new apps and delete the ones you no longer use. Voice assistant Siri answers your spoken questions and will seek information for you.

Almost everyone takes a photo once in a while with his iPhone or iPad. iOS 10 includes incredibly useful and fun ways to edit your photos. It is now possible to write on photos by hand, share them, magnify certain parts and add text blocks.

This book also deals with the topic music. You can transfer music from your PC to your iPad or iPhone, and listen to it whenever and wherever you want.

Author: Studio Visual Steps
ISBN 978 90 5905 433 2
Book type: Paperback, full color
Nr of pages: 172 pages
Accompanying website:
www.visualsteps.com/quickios10

Full color!

Learn how to:
- Use the iPad and iPhone
- Set up Touch ID and passcode
- Use the Notification Center
- Use the Control Center
- Use Email and SMS
- Use widgets
- Use apps
- Use Slide Over and Split View
- Use Siri and Spotlight
- Work with photos, video and music

Suitable for: All iPads and iPhones with iOS 10.